LENNY

LENNY

a play by
Julian Barry

**Based on the life
and words of
Lenny Bruce**

**GROVE PRESS, INC.
NEW YORK**

ISBN: 0-394-17762-2

Library of Congress Catalog Card Number: 70-185420

First Evergreen Black Cat Edition, 1972

Manufactured in the United States of America

by Colonial Press, Clinton, Massachusetts

Second Printing

Distributed by Random House, Inc., New York

"Even Socrates, for all his age and experience, did not defend himself at his trial like a man who understood the long accumulated fury that had burst on him, and was clamoring for his death; for (his accuser) had really nothing to say except that he and his like could not endure being shewn up as idiots every time Socrates opened his mouth."

—G. B. Shaw,
Preface to *St. Joan*

PERFORMANCE NOTICE

Lenny was first performed at Brooks Atkinson Theatre, New York, on May 26, 1971. Directed by Tom O'Horgan; produced by Jules Fisher, Marvin Worth, and Michael Butler; sets by Robin Wagner; costumes by Randy Barcelo; lighting by Jules Fisher; music by Tom O'Horgan; and with the following cast:

Lenny Bruce	Cliff Gorman
The Judges, Sherman Hart, General, Vampire Priest, Plainclothesman, Mr. Wollenstein, Photographer	Joe Silver
Sally, Gypsy Woman, Phone Operator	Erica Yohn
Rusty	Jane House
Juan, Primitive Drummer, Cop	Marker Bloomst
Arty, Igor, Hitler, Southern Gentleman, Photographer	Johnny Armen
Trumpet, Nod Out	Vaughn De Forest
Mema, Stripper, Lucille, R.C. Lady, Matron, Southern Lady	Jeannette Ertelt
Bass, Life Reporter, Cop	Ernie Furtado
Trombone, Nod Out	John Gordon
Saxophone, Clarinet, Flute, Nod Out	Ron Odrich

Ernie, Interviewer	Paul Lieber
Girl in Wheel Chair	Jody Oliver
Piano, Lenny's Lawyer, Eichmann	Warren Meyers
Stripper, Singer, Mrs. Hart, Secretary, Girl Without I.D. Card	Melody Santangelo
Drums, Cop	Adam Smith
Clubowner, Lenny's Father, Ike, Blah, blah Judge, D.A., Photographer	Robert Weil
Cop, Witchdoctor, Chinese Waiter, Bishop	James Wigfall

act one

☆ ☆ ☆ ☆ ☆

A monument in bathroom tiles is seen from the moment the theatre doors are open.

The rear section of the monument is draped in a huge black shroud.

In front of the shroud hangs a map of America, realized in human skins.

A WEIRD TRIBESMAN *enters and begins to beat on a drum. He is joined by* OTHER TRIBESMEN *who are beating on truck springs, hubcaps, and other assorted noise makers.*

A TOM TOM *takes over the beat, defining it more clearly, and soon* THE TRIBE *is jumping around chanting and singing as* A HUGE SHAMAN PUPPET *dances high in the air.*

TRIBE   Yadda, Yadda, Yadda, Yadda,
Yaddamop! Yaddamop!
Yaddamop, Yadda Yaddamop, Yaddamop!
Yadda Warden, Yadda Yadda Warden,
Yadda Yadda Warden, Yaddamop!
Yaddamop!
Lotta dues, Lotta dues, Lotta dues.
Yaddamop! Yaddamop!
Yaddamop, Yaddayaddamop, Yaddamop!
The nilene rappemon test the schnappemon test
The narco-busting test.

3

The nilene rappemon test
The F.B.I. and Interpol,
The nilene. . . . Yaddamop!
Yaddamop! Yaddamop!
Yaddayaddamop, Yaddamop!
Yadda Warden, Yaddayadda Warden, Yadda-
    yadda Warden,
Yaddamop! Yaddamop!
Lotta dues, Lotta dues.
Yadda Mop Mop——
Later!!!!

(*At conclusion the* SHAMAN PUPPET *has vanished and* THE BIGGEST HORN IN THE WORLD *has been brought in and blown to herald the arrival of* ONE WHO HAS HEARD FROM THE LORD.)

HEAD TRIBESMAN   All right . . . hear ye, hear ye . . . I have just heard from the Lord.

TRIBE   Yadda yadda yadda yadda.

HEAD TRIBESMAN   Pay attention now. I have spoken with the Lord and the Lord has asked that we give up things for him. Now, I'll tell you what I'm going to do. I'll start the ball rolling here. I pledge that I will give up . . . something very dear to me . . . I will give up . . . fifteen rivers and eighteen of my farms for the Lord. And that makes me the best man in the tribe!

TRIBE   Yadda yadda yadda yadda.

SECOND TRIBESMAN   I'll beat him . . . is he kidding with

that???? I'll give up seventy-five of my farms and all my cows. That's it. And that makes me the best man in the tribe.

TRIBE   Yadda yadda yadda . . .

THIRD TRIBESMAN   Just a moment. Just a moment now. I will show you all how much *I* love the Lord. *I* will give up something that will astound you . . . I will give up . . .

SECOND TRIBESMAN   Go ahead . . . say it.

THIRD TRIBESMAN   No . . . I don't want to say the word.

HEAD TRIBESMAN   Oh . . . then write it down someplace.

SECOND TRIBESMAN   Yeah . . . here's a writing down thing.

HEAD TRIBESMAN   Put it down here.

> (SECOND TRIBESMAN *brings a slate and* THIRD TRIBESMAN *writes.* SECOND TRIBESMAN *brings slate to* FIRST TRIBESMAN *who reads it . . . impressed. Rest of* TRIBE *read over his shoulder.*)

TRIBE   Yadda yadda yadda yadda . . .

FIRST TRIBESMAN   Oh, come on now . . . are you kidding with that?

ANOTHER   You're giving that up just to prove a point? You're out of your mind.

ANOTHER   How long you giving it up for?

THIRD TRIBESMAN   For ever and ever.

ANOTHER   Well, go beat that . . . now he's the best man in the tribe.

ANOTHER   That's right . . . cause he gave that up for the Lord.

SECOND TRIBESMAN   Now wait a minute. I don't intend to give that up.

ANOTHER   Oh, you gave that up a long time ago.

SECOND TRIBESMAN   But what about the people who don't give it up?

HEAD TRIBESMAN   That makes them second best. That's how the scale works.

ANOTHER   Well, what about the people who talk about it?

TRIBE   Yadda yadda yadda . . .

HEAD TRIBESMAN   The people who do what?

ANOTHER   The people who talk about "doing it." What about them?

HEAD TRIBESMAN We'll just . . . *bust their ass*. And talking about it will be dirty . . . dirty . . . dirty . . .

TRIBE *(as they go off)* Dirty . . . dirty . . . dirty . . . dirty . . .

LENNY *(offstage mike)* Lenny Bruce, ladies and gentlemen . . . Lenny Bruce.

(TRIBE *clears as* LENNY *comes out and grabs club mike*.) *Six* CLUB MUSICIANS *cluster around bandstand and crack up at the following.*

LENNY Thank you . . . thank you . . . I just got finished playing in a town called Lima, Ohio. I don't know whether you people have ever worked in a small town . . . if there are any salesmen here tonight you'll know what I'm talking about. There's nothing to do in these places. First day in a small town, you go to the park, you see the cannon, and you've had it. Second day . . . you give your picture to the delicatessen, if you can find a delicatessen . . . "Maurice, thanks for the lean brisket, Lenny." Right next to Shep Fields and his gourds. Things are so bad in these places you get into a cab, the driver turns around and asks you if you know a place where *he* can get laid. Culture changes in small towns . . . and very innocently, too. They have big signs, like . . . you know the Italian submarine sandwiches . . . those hero sandwiches on French bread . . . They'll have signs like: "Don's Big Dago, 35¢" . . . and think nothing of that. I picture one of those poor guys coming to New York . . . going down to Mulberry Street, to one of those scungilli stands, run by the Brothers Nunzio . . . "Yeah, whatta ya want?" . . . "Oh, hi, give me a big dago, please." . . . "I'll give you a big dago, ya bastid" . . . POW . . . Right in the head. A lobotomy and a chest X-ray, one shot. Really weird. Okay, well, here I am, playing in Baltimore. And I figure . . . now, this place is really going to swing. Nada. Know what I've been doing ever since I got here . . . going to the movies. But every theatre in town is showing a different version of the same dopey flick . . . *Prison Break* . . . "Inside the Walls of Wholesome Prison" . . . Let me show you what I mean. I would like to take you now to . . . *Prison Break* . . . that same movie that we've all seen a hundred times . . . because it's been made a hundred times . . . starring Charles Bickford, George E. Stone, Frankie Darrow, Warren Hymer, Turhan Bey and the woman across the bay, Ann Dvorak, and her two hooker friends . . . Iris Adrian and Arlene Dahl . . . there in the prison yard where the convicts are rioting and eighteen prison guards are being held hostage. The warden's in his tower . . .

(WARDEN) All right, Dutch. This is the warden. You've got eighteen men down there, prison guards who've served me faithfully for many years. Give up, Dutch, and we will meet any reasonable demands you've got . . . except for the vibrators . . . forget it, men . . . you're not getting them.

(DUTCH) Yadda yadda yadda yadda Warden. Yadda yadda yadda.

(WARDEN) Never mind those Louis Armstrong imitations, Dutch. You'd better give up. You're a rotten, vicious criminal.

(DUTCH)   Yadda yadda yadda . . .

(WARDEN)   Shut up, you goddamn nut you. Yaddayaddayadda. I'm sorry I gave him that library card. Moron. I dunno what to do with these guys . . . maybe if we kill about four or five for an example. Get me Tower C. Hello, Tower C? Kill about fifteen down there . . . the bullets? Call my wife . . . they're in the back of my brown slacks. Come on now, don't put me on. The ones in the gray shirts . . . you know which ones to kill.

(FATHER FLOTSKY/BARRY FITZGERALD)   Just a moment. Before there's any killing, I'd better get down there.

(WARDEN)   Not you, Father Flotsky.

(FATHER FLOTSKY)   Yes . . . I'm going down there.

(WARDEN)   Father, you don't understand. Those guys are monsters, they've got knives and guns.

(FATHER FLOTSKY)   Son, you seem to forget that there are things stronger than knives and guns.

(WARDEN)   Do you mean . . . ?

(FATHER FLOTSKY)   That's right . . . Jujitsu.

(HIMSELF)   Now, the handsome but eccentric prison doctor, Sabu.

(SABU, *sings*)   "I want to be a sailor." (*Speaks.*) They hate you. You're corrupt. That's why the men hate

you and cut you. That is not the way to kill people. That is why the men cut the men up. My father don't know to do that.

(WARDEN)   Get outta here, you big pill head, you.
Take your turban with you.

(HIMSELF)   Meanwhile, back in the yard . . .

(FATHER FLOTSKY)   Hello, Dutch. You don't remember Father Flotsky, do you? You don't. Do you remember Arthur Shields for Italian Swiss Colony
Wine? Neither of the above, I see. Think of me as
a passing priest. Now, you're not a bad boy. Killing six children doesn't make you all bad. Come
on, give me the gun, Dutch.

(DUTCH)   Yaddayaddayadda . . .

(FATHER FLOTSKY)   Come on, give me the gun.

(DUTCH)   Get outta heah, faddah.

(FATHER FLOTSKY)   Give me the gun, Dutch . . . the
Rabbi's watching.

(HIMSELF)   Now we cut to death row. Little Abie, the
East Side Jewish kid, is gonna get burned tonight.

(ABIE, *sings*)   I'm gwine up ta hebben on dat big rib-
baboat.

(VOICE)   Them Jews is always singing, man.

(HYSTERICAL VOICE)   I don't wanna die . . . I don't
wanna die . . . I don't wanna die . . . I don't
wanna die . . .

(ANOTHER VOICE)   Schmuck . . . you're a guard.

(HYSTERICAL VOICE) I'm a guard . . . I'm not gonna die. Right! Okay!

(HIMSELF) Meanwhile, back at the warden's tower . . .

(WARDEN) All right, you mean . . . the prison guards. Look, I dunno what this is, but Dutch don't wanna give up and I got an election coming up and ah, it's dog eat dog, you know what I mean? Dutch, c'mon now, don't be crazy. Give up. You got two seconds. Listen to me now.

(DUTCH) I ain't gonna listen to nobody. Nobody in this whole rotten stinkin' prison.

(KIKI) Dutch, lithen to me, bubby.

(DUTCH) Who is that?

(KIKI) It's me, Kiki, the hospital attendant. Don't schtup your good time. Give up for me and I'll make a new life for us.

(DUTCH) Kiki . . . you nafka you. All right. I'll give it all up for you.

(KIKI) Woo . . . give it up for me. I feel like Wally Simpson. Did you hear that all you bitches in cell block eleven? Did you hear that Warden?

(WARDEN) Yeah, I heard him, ya fag bastid.

(KIKI) Are we going to get our demands?

(WARDEN) Whaddya want, you fruit?

(KIKI) Well . . . we want a gay bar in the west wing.

(WARDEN) Yeah . . .

(KIKI)   And one more thing.

(WARDEN)   What's that?

(KIKI)   I wanna be the Avon representative for this prison.

(*Big hand from band.* CLUBOWNER *enters and band moves around* LENNY.)

CLUBOWNER   What is this . . . what is this? What are you rehearsing? You're not going to do that in my club, are you?

LENNY   I stayed up all night in the hotel working on that. Let me try it the second show.

CLUBOWNER   You outta your mind? You want me to get arrested? You want me to lose my license? You can't talk like that. Making fun of priests. Talking about queers in prison . . . and vibrators. (*To band.*) Hey, c'mon fellas . . . into the kitchen . . . it's show time. (*To* LENNY.) Hey, Lenny . . . you know who's in my club tonight?

LENNY   Yeah. Sherman Hart. I invited him.

(SHERMAN HART *is seen suddenly as he poses with a polio victim in a wheelchair.*)

CLUBOWNER   Well, maybe you'll do a decent show, then. I mean . . . Christ, Lenny . . . what happened last night?

LENNY   I don't know, man . . . it was granite out there

. . . Washington, Jefferson, Lincoln . . . fifty people staring up at me . . . an oil painting . . .

CLUBOWNER   You know why? I'll tell ya, Lenny . . . see I bought you for the surefire imitations . . . Cagney, Vaughn Monroe . . . not little throwaway lines to the band. I mean . . . you know I'm hep, Lenny, but this is Baltimore and they don't understand your Louis Armstrong imitation . . .

LENNY   Don't hack me, man . . . you'll have a dynamite second show, okay?

> (LENNY *is no longer paying attention. He is diverted by the sight of a* STRIPPER *in a red wig and the sounds of strip music.* LENNY *drifts over and watches. She finishes her strip, removes the wig, and becomes an old lady and the catcher.* SECOND STRIPPER *appears in the same kind of wig. Throws her stuff to* FIRST STRIPPER. *Racy* RUSTY INGRAM *enters, stripping. She has great red hair, a great body, and a face that's a cross between the Virgin Mary and a five-hundred-dollar-a-night hooker.* LENNY *goes over to her as she works.*)

I don't think I ever saw anything as wild as when you walked into the delicatessen tonight. Everybody just stopped chewing . . . and then when you dropped your fork and looked at me . . . I wigged right out of my head. I hadda meet you.

RUSTY   Yeah. I dug meeting you, too.

LENNY I wanted to get you over to the club to see me perform . . . not because I'm so crazy about my act . . .
but I had to figure out some way to see you again.

RUSTY Oh, I was hip, daddy.

LENNY Yeah . . . that face of yours . . . I've always been
a sucker for that German-Irish face. You midwestern
chicks are really winner chicks.

RUSTY Oh, I'm so glad you feel that way.

(LENNY *takes* RUSTY *to table in club and* SHERMAN
joins them.)

LENNY (*to* RUSTY *as* THEY *go*) Now, the question is . . .
how do I get you away from Sherman Hart?

SHERMAN There is absolutely no question in my mind,
Lenny, we got to stop that Stalin now . . . I mean . . .
if we let the Reds take over South Korea . . . next thing
you know . . . right? And not only that, Lenny, but you
know this war has saved the nightclub business.

LENNY You mind if I use that for an opening gag, Sherman?

SHERMAN Go ahead . . . take it. Hey . . . did you hear
the one about the two cannibals . . . one of them said,
"I hate my mother-in-law." And the other one said, "So,
just eat the noodles." Killed them at the Concord with
that one. Listen, Lenny, what are you doing after the
show?

LENNY (*looking at* RUSTY) Well, I don't know . . . I was
. . . ah . . .

SHERMAN Well come with us, Lenny. The little lady and
myself are going to a party . . . just a bunch of local
hood action . . . but they like show people . . . they're
really nice guys and they're good friends of mine . . .
(*Writes on a matchbook cover at the same time* LENNY *is
making signs to* RUSTY *to call him later on the telephone.*)
. . . here . . . and what the hell . . . the food is always
good at those places . . .

LENNY Well, I'll think it over, Sherman . . . actually I
promised the band I'd go up to Wilmington with them
after the gig. Dizzy is supposed to show up at a jam ses-
sion later on and they . . .

SHERMAN Dizzy? Dizzy Dean?

RUSTY No . . . Gillespie.

LENNY There you go! (*Getting up—to* RUSTY.) Excuse me.
I want to get something straight with the band, so I'm
going *backstage* for a while . . . I'll see you later, okay?

RUSTY (*with an understanding nod*) Okay . . . great.

LENNY (*on his way out spots his mother sitting at a table*)
Momma! (*Hugs his mother who whispers something in his
ear that cracks him up.*)

SALLY I'm the only one who can make my son Lenny
laugh.

(LENNY *goes to an area where the band is sharing a joint.*)

FIRST MUSICIAN   Hey, Lenny . . . ain't that the chick from the deli?

LENNY   Yeah, she's with Sherman Hart.

SECOND MUSICIAN   He playin' in town?

LENNY   He's got a new disease he's pushing . . . polio . . . but don't give to the *other* polio . . . just to *his* polio. But did you dig that chick he's with?

FIRST MUSICIAN   Oh, Christ . . . you're not going to make Wilmington with us, are you?

(*By now* RUSTY *has slipped away from the table and found a phone and dialed. It rings.* JUAN (*a busboy*) *picks it up.*)

JUAN   Lenny, it's for dju.

LENNY (*taking phone from* JUAN)   This is the kitchen of the Club Charles.

RUSTY   Hi.

LENNY   Oh, listen . . . if I do something really outrageous to get rid of Sherman . . . is that going to screw you up in any way?

RUSTY   Well, like, what do you mean?

LENNY   I don't know . . . I'll kill him if you want me to.

RUSTY   However you want to handle it, man. Just as long as he doesn't get hurt.

LENNY   All right. I'll work it out. Some way. It'll be hip. You'll dig it.

RUSTY   Okay. Later.

(*She hangs up and goes back to table.* LENNY *grabs a joint away from someone in the band.*)

LENNY   Did you hear me? "I'll kill him if you want me to." I tell you . . . chicks are really . . . powerful . . . the power that chicks have . . .

CLUBOWNER (*busting it up*)   Come on . . . what's going on here . . . the show is out there, boys. (*To* BUSBOY—*same tone of voice.*) You, clear those tables off, will ya?

FIRST MUSICIAN (*as he goes*)   Hey, Lenny . . . do that "Prison Break" bit anyway—that's dynamite . . .

LENNY   Can't, man . . .

CLUBOWNER   Hey, wait a minute, Lenny . . . what are you gonna do out there?

LENNY   Oh, man . . . what are you so nervous about? I mean, it's only a nightclub, all right???!

CLUBOWNER (*grabs a backstage mike—looks at* LENNY *ner-*

vously) Ladies and gentlemen . . . Baltimore's Club Charles proudly presents America's fastest rising young comedian . . . direct from his big win on the Arthur Godfrey Talent Scouts program . . . the wonderful impressions of Lenny Bruce.

(*Band hits it.* LENNY *appears. As* CLUBOWNER *watches nervously,* LENNY *grabs mike.*)

LENNY (*out front—as* CHEVALIER) Good evening ladies and gentlemen . . . hohoho . . . usualleee I would seeng for you a leetle song about a leetle girl name Mee Mee, but we have een theee club tonight one of the great personality of all time . . . Meeester Sherman Hart . . .

(*Big hand.* SHERMAN *rises.*)

(HIMSELF) Stand up and take a bow, Sherman . . . come on up and do a few minutes.

SHERMAN No . . . I couldn't.

LENNY Come on . . . it would be a pleasure to hear you work. Sherman Hart, ladies and gentlemen . . .

SHERMAN (*leaping for the floor and practically knocking* LENNY *off*) Thank you, ladies and gentlemen . . . it's really a thrill to be here in Baltimore. As you all know, we're in town doing a benefit for polio. Ladies and gentlemen, today I had the privilege of having my picture taken with one of those wonderful kids . . . I'm here to

tell you they can really break your heart . . . because
they're so . . . brave . . . about the whole thing . . .

> (*During this,* LENNY *has drifted off and signaled*
> RUSTY *to drift off. They drift to a bed.*)

I tell ya though, folks, I just got back from a really crazy
town . . . a crazy crazy place . . . Lost Wages, Nevada
. . . Funny thing about working Lost Wages, Nevada
. . . the way to make a lot of money there . . . when
you get off the plane, walk right into the propeller . . .

> (*Audience laughs.* RUSTY *is lying on bed in a hotel
> room asleep.* LENNY *is watching her.*)

Meanwhile, General MacArthur's *mother-in-law* . . .

> (*Audience laughs.*)

. . . says that the U.S. 24th Division has all checked
into a *motel* . . .

> (*Audience laughs.*)

. . . and has plugged up the hole in the line with a *min-
ister, a priest, and a rabbi* . . .

> (*Audience laughs.*)

. . . meantime a little pansy is fighting a gallant holding action at the rail junction of Taejon.

(Audience laughs. Sherman's voice merges with that of a customer at a table who leans into a radio mike and becomes a RADIO ANNOUNCER.*)*

RADIO ANNOUNCER   In a follow-up to his press conference of yesterday, President Truman reemphasized that . . .

SHERMAN *(as* TRUMAN*)*   The United States is not at war. We are merely involved in a "police action."

LENNY   Bullshit, Harry.

RADIO ANNOUNCER   The President also served notice that he has allowed the U.S. Airforce to bomb specific military targets inside North Korea. Commenting on the situation, General Dwight D. Eisenhower stated . . .

SHERMAN *(as* EISENHOWER*)*   You can't win anywhere if you don't win this one.

LENNY   That's pretty hep, Ike. (SHERMAN *vanishes.* LENNY *studies Rusty's almost naked body.*) Aghn. I gotta get the fuck out of Baltimore. (*He starts putting things in a ditty bag and finds a box of Trojans. Studies it. Takes one out.*) I always go through the trouble to buy you things and then I forget to use you. Actually I don't really forget . . . I like . . . blot it out . . . (*Blows it up and studies it.*) Why, it's the Hindenberg! She's arriving at Lakehurst, New Jersey. The mooring mast is ready. The mooring lines are down . . . oh, my god . . . it burst into flames. The Hindenberg's exploded . . . oh, the humanity . . .

(His FATHER *appears suddenly.)*

FATHER What is that? You've been in my top drawer again, right?

LENNY No . . . I . . . owwww . . . what are you hitting me for?

FATHER Because you know too damn much already. Now go outside. They're just balloons. But they're *mine*. Now get outside and get some air. (FATHER *vanishes.*)

LENNY I don't know . . . I could put on a Mary Jane or some bubble gum, but I just can't wear a balloon.

RUSTY Lenny?

LENNY Yeah?

RUSTY What are you doing? Come back to bed.

LENNY Yes, dear. Soon as I put on my balloon. (*He lets it deflate. Picks it up.*) No . . . it's impossible. (*He drops it and goes back to her.*)

RUSTY Hey . . . what are you doing out of bed?

LENNY I had to make a sissy.

RUSTY So come back to bed.

LENNY Aghn . . . no . . . listen. I gotta talk to you. I gotta go home.

RUSTY Why?

LENNY   Well, it's time . . . you know.

RUSTY   You got an engagement somewhere?

LENNY   Yeah . . . Montreal. I can always go back to Montreal. Where can I get in touch with you?

RUSTY (*putting his hand on her breast*)   Right here.

LENNY   Cool it. I mean . . . where are you going from here?

RUSTY   Did you mean what you said or was it just the tea we smoked?

LENNY   Is there a number . . . your agent or someone who knows where I can reach you?

RUSTY   Hey, come on, man. You laid a big sound on me last night in this bed, and I want to know if you were kidding. I mean you said some pretty crazy things, Lenny.

LENNY (*a long sigh—then*)   . . . I know . . .

RUSTY   It was all crap, right?

LENNY   No. I'm out of my mind over you. Completely wigged out. I don't know what I'm doing anymore. (*Out front.*) See, here's the hangup: I was in the Navy in World War Two, and so I've been halfway around the world and I've balled all kinds of chicks, but never . . . until now . . . have I spent a whole week sleeping with a woman. And it's really nice. And this chick is really making me crazy because she's got that certain goyishe thing that just whacks me out of my mind. Shiksas. You know, it's not that Jewish girls are not attractive to me, but it's just that pink-nippled, freckled goyishe punim . . . that is hot . . . Boy, that is a rare tribe. But see, I know that hotel rooms are deceptive. It's easy to be happy in a hotel room in a weird city with a strange chick . . . (*Turns to* RUSTY.) You understand? No cooking. No garbage. No furniture that has anything to do with either of us . . . complete illusion . . . complete fantasy.

RUSTY   So what's wrong with a little fantasy?

LENNY   Nothing, but . . .

RUSTY   I love you, Lenny Bruce, I love you . . . you're so damned funny, man, and you make me feel so great . . . come on, Daddy . . . ball me.

LENNY   Ball you? Yeah, I'd like to spend the rest of my life balling you.

RUSTY   So what's stopping you?

LENNY   My head . . . my head keeps telling me this is insane.

RUSTY   Yeah, but like . . . my heart hurts, man . . . and it never hurt me before.

LENNY   Come on.

RUSTY   Where?

LENNY   We're going to Brooklyn.

RUSTY   Brooklyn?

LENNY   Yeah. I want you to meet two really flipped out people.

RUSTY   Who?

LENNY   My mother and my aunt.

> (*He goes to* RUSTY, *helps her get into her shoes, and leads her to where* SALLY *and his Aunt* MEMA *are waiting over a dinner.*)

SALLY   Oh, look at that face. Isn't she beautiful?

LENNY   You dig that face? . . . That's a cross between the Virgin Mary and a five-hundred-dollar-a-night hooker.

MEMA   Sadie. Serve.

RUSTY   I thought your name was Sally.

LENNY   Sadie Kitchenberg. Alias Sally Marr. And on your right is Leonard Alfred Schneider, alias Lenny Bruce. Aunt Mema is the only one here without a phony name, right?

MEMA   So, I'm not in the comedy business.

LENNY   And you're not "Racy" Rusty Ingram, either. (*As* CAGNEY.) Come on, baby . . . out wid it.

RUSTY   Jane.

LENNY   Jane what?

RUSTY   (*a pretty good* MAE WEST) Well, big boy, that's somethin' ya gonna have ta find out fa yaself.

SALLY   (*as* DURANTE) Everybody wants ta get inta de act.

MEMA   Shh. Eat. What do you do, Miss?

SALLY   I told you, Mema . . . she's a . . . exotic dancer. You know, Mema, like Minsky's . . . (*She's on.*) Say Lenny, Lenny . . . you know, that gives me a crazy idea for a bit . . . like I'm up there doing my act, right, and joke joke joke and suddenly I give it a fast . . . "Okay boys . . . you're bored with the comic . . . here's the stripper . . . here's Sadie Kitchenberg." (*Opens her dress to reveal stripper outfit.*)

LENNY   How do you like it so far? A little weird, right?

RUSTY   Oh, I love it. It's so . . . honest.

MEMA   So, are you two getting married?

SALLY   Mema, what are you nudging for?

MEMA   I'm asking questions.

SALLY   Seriously though . . . how long have you kids known each other?

LENNY   About half an hour.

RUSTY   Lenny!

LENNY   Yeah. She was sitting on the D train in this empty car . . . there was no one else around, so I . . . (*Pantomimes a guy exposing himself.*)

MEMA   (*hitting him, with a scream like a Jewish seagull*)   Feh, Lenny!!!!

SALLY   You think it's funny, Lenny . . . but yesterday a guy . . . (*picks up lid of serving dish*) right out at the bus stop . . . (*covers her crotch with lid*) . . .

LENNY   Hello dere!!!

SALLY (*flashing with the lid*)   . . . yeah . . . with *The New York Times.*

MEMA   And this morning . . . a bum . . . (*notices* SALLY *putting the lid back to its original use*) . . . not with the milchadich . . . (*takes the contaminated lid off the dish*) . . . a filthy bum . . . undid himself just as I'm coming out of the elevator!

LENNY (*out front*)   I can't stand it. This is the reason why I would never have the nerve to talk to a strange chick on the street . . . *ever* . . . because all I remember from my childhood is my mother and aunt coming home with stories about some guy who was always jumping out of a bush somewhere exposing himself. And it really has me hung up. You know, after a while I finally figured out it was just a dopey lie . . . and they were trying to tell me that they were good, good women, right?

SALLY Oh, he doesn't believe us . . . because they never do it to *him* . . . but you probably see that all the time . . . from the stage . . . right, Rusty?

RUSTY Well . . . yes and no.

MEMA Feh! They should be killed!!!

LENNY (*out front*) So I said . . . "Mema, Mema, you've already killed hundreds with that big black pocketbook of yours" . . . you know, with that Jewish seagull scream of hers . . . "Fehhhhhhhh," "Fehhhhhhhh." I mean . . . to hear them tell it you would think there was a band of dedicated perverts who spend their whole life in trick positions just waiting for them. (*Does some fast variations, with gestures, as* ARTIE *and* ERNIE, *two close friends, appear.*) Hey lady . . . yoooohooooo . . . okay . . . hey . . .

ARTIE Look this way, lady . . . over here in the bushes.

ERNIE Yeah . . . find the schmuck in the bush.

LENNY Okay boys . . . it's almost two o'clock. Sally and Mema are due . . . oil up your zippers . . . Artie, you take the elevator . . . Ernie, you got the bus . . . I'll take the subway . . . that's all they got to do all day, right? (*They are all falling out, laughing.*) What a bit! I swear to God, I'm gonna do that on the floor some night.

ERNIE   You crazy?

ARTIE   Forget it!

ERNIE   Blue material!

ARTIE   You'll get killed for it, Lenny!

LENNY   I know and that's what kills me, man. Jokes, jokes . . . meaningless jokes is what my life is all about.

ARTIE   Yeah, but we worked like bastards . . . the Strand . . . Broadway Open House . . . you gotta swing with your career now or forget it.

LENNY   Career. Career. What a weird choice of words. Throwing jokes in some toilet. You know . . . a Doctor . . . a lawyer . . . a chiropractor . . . that's a career.

ARTIE   Look, Lenny. I know that this chick is making you crazy . . . what do you say I book you into Montreal for a couple of weeks?

LENNY   Montreal?

ARTIE   You'll make some bread and have time to think everything out. What do you say, Lenny?

LENNY   No. No . . . I've got a hipper idea.

(*Stripper music. A strip club is seen.*)

ERNIE   But Lenny . . . you can't marry that stripper.

ARTIE   Ernie, will you shut up with "can't" . . . that's the
wrong word *always* to say to Lenny, man.

(RUSTY *is seen stripping.* LENNY *looks at her a moment and then, making a lightning decision, he leaps
up on the stage.* RUSTY'*s mouth falls open. Customers
begin to shout at him.* LENNY *pulls out a wallet and
flips it open.*)

LENNY   All right . . . Vice Squad . . . get out your I.D.'s.

RUSTY   Lenny!

LENNY   This girl is only fourteen years old, and you're all
under arrest for staring at her nay nays. Don't try to
leave, the block is cordoned off. All right, Mulligan . . .
get the tear gas and the riot guns . . . Who's in charge
here?

(LENNY *starts to pull her off, sees the* CLUBOWNER
*rushing onstage angrily, and cuts out into the club
with* RUSTY. *People start to run for exits and the
band is packing up and leaving hastily.*)

CLUBOWNER   Hey, wait a minute, now . . . I just paid off
. . . You people are bleeding me to death.

LENNY   You heard him. Trying to bribe an officer . . .
Get the handcuffs.

CLUBOWNER (*copping out*) No . . . listen, I'm not the owner . . . I'm just the manager . . . My wife is the owner.

> (LENNY *has worked his way through the confusion and is heading for an exit.* BASS PLAYER *passes* LENNY *and* LENNY *yells to him.*)

LENNY   You better put the choir on for ten minutes.

RUSTY   Lenny, are you crazy . . . I'm gonna get fired.

LENNY   You are fired.

RUSTY   Where are you taking me?

LENNY (*as* DRACULA) To the soil of my native homeland . . . Traaannnnsssyyyllvannia.

RUSTY   Come on, Lenny . . . where?

LENNY   Somewhere over the rainbow.

RUSTY   Oh yeah?

LENNY   Yeah . . . way up high . . . someplace beautiful where you won't have to strip and I won't have to tell jokes.

RUSTY   So what do we do for bread?

LENNY   I don't know . . . we'll work it out.

RUSTY Come on. I want to know where we're going, Lenny.

LENNY Into a whole new beautiful insane thing. California, baby!

> (*Wedding music.* SHERMAN *appears as a black magic rabbi.* ARTIE *and* ERNIE *enter and put Dracula capes around* RUSTY *and* LENNY.)

SHERMAN Do you, Leonard Alfred Schneider . . . take this woman, Racy Rusty Ingram, to be your lawful wedded wife?

LENNY (*as* DRACULA) Permmmittt me to say I do.

RUSTY I do.

ARTIE *and* ERNIE We do, too.

LENNY I vill love her and suck her neck. And never vill I chippy on her and suck anyone else's neck.

SHERMAN All right. Agreed?

RUSTY, ARTIE, ERNIE, LENNY Agreed.

SHERMAN All right. Then you have my permission to go to the West Coast of the United States and make new lives for yourselves . . . and be happily ever after. But I warn you. Do not suck blood indiscriminately.

(*ARTIE suddenly doubles over and becomes* IGOR, *a hunchback cripple.*)

And so . . . they made their way unto the Coast, spending one last night in Brooklyn. Wow!

(*SALLY appears as* MARIA OUSPENSKAYA.)

SALLY Who are you, young man? I've never seen your face before. Are you a stranger to Transylvania?

LENNY Permmmmmmitttt me to introduce myself. Hahahaha.

SALLY Oh, you come on pretty wild. What's your name?

LENNY My name is Count Dracula, and we are looking for lodgings for the night . . . myself . . . my dumb friend . . . and my wife . . .

SALLY She's your wife? That Shiksa? (*Putting* RUSTY *into a trance with a gesture that causes lightning to strike.*) Feh!

LENNY Cool it, Sadie. Ve are but a small showbiz troupe on our way to the Coast and ve are very pleasant people.

ARTIE/IGOR (*as* BORIS KARLOFF) But Master . . . you promised to straighten out my hunch. You promised years ago when I came to the laboratory.

LENNY Shut up . . . I'll punch you in the hunch. Pock! (*Punches him in the hunch.*) And don't bug me no more.

You look groovy that way. Look at the money we made on the parties at Fire Island with those freaks looking at you . . .

SALLY Well, I heard about you show people, and it's customary that we get a little gelt in advance.

LENNY I'm a little hung for bread right now, but ah . . . Igor, vengaca.

ARTIE Si?

LENNY Perhaps you'd like to punch Igor in the hunch?

SALLY Well, I've never done anything so weird before . . . but . . .

LENNY Yes. There is a whole chapter on this in Krafft-Ebing.

SALLY Haha. I'm not a freak. Teehee. Oh, but . . . I remember years ago, when the Woody Herman Band was through here . . . Stan Getz . . . Zoot Sims . . . Hahahahahahaha. I'll never be the same again.

LENNY All right . . . then you can punch Igor in the hunch.

ARTIE Now wait a minute, Master. I don't intend to get punched in the hunch clear across the country.

LENNY All right, then, stay in New York and manage comics. I am fed up with you. (ARTIE *limps out, cursing in*

Yiddish.) And now, old woman. Here is ten pieces of bat shit. And don't bug me no more. Freak. (*She goes.* LENNY *turns to* RUSTY.) Now I will take my wife out of her trance. (*He makes some insane gestures at her.*) Wake up. It is time to suck necks.

RUSTY (*a cross between a naggy, Jewish wife and Anastasia*) That's all you think about, you degenerate, you. Agh. I can't stand to look at you anymore. Phah! You know what it means when a woman can't stand to look at a man anymore? Our knot is gone, Bela. The stake is burned out.

LENNY All right, get off my back, you vitch. You band rat. Sure, hanging around Birdland always. Everybody freaked off vit you. And I vas nice enough to take you avay from all dot.

> (*The argument rages on, but they drop the Dracula accents and capes and* RUSTY *is in stripper's outfit once more and they seem in each other's way. They are in a West Coast apartment, with a Christmas tree and presents.*)

RUSTY Oh sure. Turn your back on the truth. Go get high with the band. Go on . . . shoot up with the drummer.

LENNY Me shoot up with the drummer? That's a hot one. You should talk. I learned that one from you.

RUSTY Never mind. I know what's bugging you.

LENNY So . . . a couple of pills. Don't hack me about it.

RUSTY   I just don't understand you, Lenny, that's all. They offered me good bread in Vegas.

LENNY   I'm not sitting around some motel pool in Vegas while my old lady strips.

RUSTY   Well, we're dying out here in L.A. as a duo, Lenny, let's face it. I'm not a singer, Lenny, and we can't live off club dates in Bakersfield. This is a shitty town to be broke in. And I'm only going to be able to go on working a few more months, so I better make it while I can. (*He doesn't respond.*) Well, don't you wanna know why? (*No response.*) Because you don't want to wear a balloon, that's why. (*Waits.*) Well??? (*Nothing.*) Okay, then you can decorate the tree the way you want to. (*Knocks the tree over.*) Come on, Lenny. What's your smart-ass reply to that?

LENNY   Nada. (*She exits; he sings like Mel Torme.*)

> I'll be . . .
> All Alone
> What a joy
> Don't you see,
> I've convinced you, now how about me?

(*spoken*) I'll get my own pad. I'll really swing. I know how to fix up a pad. I'll get a hifi stereo, a bullfight poster and a black coffee table. No! I'll get a coffee table and make a door out of it. (*He has drifted into something representing a Chinese restaurant. Sings.*)

> No more taking out the garbage,
> Hear her yacking on the phone.

When I'm rich and famous
She'll be sorry . . .
All alone
All alone
All . . .
Alone.

(*A Chinese* WAITER *appears and fawns over* LENNY.)

WAITER   Ah, so . . . verrry good from Column A. Where's maw maw? How come you don't bring maw maw in? Maw maw most wonderful wife I ever see. What's a matter? Maw maw sick? Ah, so. You better bring maw maw home some fortune cookies. She wonderful wife.

LENNY   I'm divorced.

WAITER (*suddenly coming on like* PEARL BAILEY)   Baby, you better off!

LENNY   Christ, that's really "go with the winner." You better off!

(*Trumpet is heard reaching for high notes. Another Christmas tree (this one pink flocked) is seen, as well as a crib.* LENNY *walks into the area where three musicians are sitting around near the tree. The* TRUMPET PLAYER *is doing high register exercises. A* WOMAN *who takes care of the* CHILD *comes over to* LENNY.)

WOMAN Mr. Bruce. It's time for the baby's nap.

LENNY (*to* TRUMPET PLAYER) Hey, you want to cool that, man.

> (ARTIE *looks around with displeasure noting that one of the musicians looks really spaced and another has nodded out on the floor.*)

WOMAN I'm going out now, Mr. Bruce.

LENNY Okay, Lucille . . . thanks . . . don't worry, I'll see that she gets her nap, okay? (*The* NOD-OUT CAT *comes to life and turns to* ARTIE.)

NOD-OUT You just make the Coast, man?

ARTIE Yeah, Saturday.

NOD-OUT You'll dig it here . . . it's like so much healthier out here than in . . . like . . . in . . . ah . . . (*He nods out after a vague gesture in the general direction of New York.*)

ARTIE Yeah . . . they say it's a great place to bring up kids. (TRUMPET PLAYER *begins playing again.*)

LENNY For Chrissake, man . . .

TRUMPET PLAYER That stripper music is really wreckin' my chops.

LENNY Look . . . I went through tortures to get custody of the kid . . . and it's up to me to see that she gets something resembling a normal life . . . like a nap, all right? (*Turns to* ARTIE.) Hey, you want to see her do some bits before she falls out?

ARTIE I'd love to.

> (LENNY *and* ARTIE *make their way to the crib followed by the two awake musicians. They all peer into the crib.*)

LENNY Say goodnight to all your weird uncles, baby.

> (TRUMPET PLAYER *holds fingers to his lips and buzzes a little rock-a-bye-baby.*)

Enough . . . the kid is shitting and he's doing Miles Davis to her.

> (*Telephone rings.*)

ARTIE Want me to get it, Lenny?

LENNY No, I know who it is. (*He grabs a phone.*)

OPERATOR'S VOICE Hello? Mr. Bruce? I have a collect call from a Mrs. Rusty Bruce in Honolulu.

LENNY Okay, yeah. Let me know when it's three minutes, operator. (RUSTY *is seen lying on a bed, strung out.*)

OPERATOR'S VOICE   Ready on your call to the mainland, Miss. Hello. Hello. Are you there, Miss?

LENNY (*shouting*)   Rusty!!

RUSTY   Lenny?

LENNY   Yeah.

RUSTY   What's shaking? What do you want?

LENNY   What do *I* want? You called me.

RUSTY   Oh, right. What are you doing?

LENNY   Just getting ready to go to the gig.

RUSTY   Where you working?

LENNY   Duffy's. M.C.'ing strippers.

RUSTY   Well, listen . . . my lawyer says I may have to go to jail on this Narco rap. I already owe him a lotta bread. Can you help me out, man?

LENNY   I'll do what I can.

RUSTY   How's the baby?

LENNY   Fine. Just fine.

RUSTY   Do you change her a lot? You gotta change her a lot or she gets those rashes.

LENNY   Yeah, I'm hip.

RUSTY (*after a pause*)   . . . Lenny? . . .

LENNY   Yeah, I'm still here, but I gotta hang up. I can't deal with these phone bills . . . it just never stops. Have your lawyer write me and send me his bill, okay?

OPERATOR   Ready on your call to the mainland, Miss.

LENNY   What do you mean "ready"? I've been on the phone for half an hour already and you were going to tell me when it was three minutes.

OPERATOR   Well, there's no need to get nasty, sir.

RUSTY   Well, I gotta hang up now, Daddy. Merry Christmas. Talk to ya soon.

LENNY   Yeah . . . Merry Christmas. (*They hang up.* LENNY *stands frozen a moment, brooding. Suddenly the* TRUMPET PLAYER *starts in again.* LENNY *flips out.*) Will you get the hell out of here, you moron??? All of you . . . split. Like . . . later . . . all right?

TRUMPET PLAYER   What are you getting so salty about?

LENNY   I'm sorry, man, later, ha?

(*They go.* ARTIE *studies* LENNY *for a while, then.*)

ARTIE   How is she?

LENNY Fucked up. She's just like me . . . fucked up good. (*Movie trailer time.*) He was a lower-middle-class Jewish boy who thought he could find happiness married to the heroine of his nocturnal emissions . . . Together they would defy the world and swing and have a ball . . . But all they got was . . . fucked up . . . Starring Glenda Farrell and Sabu! Yeah, that's it, man. I'm a prisoner in a goddamn B movie.

ARTIE Goddamn you, Lenny. You know, yesterday I was with Ernie . . . in his cabana at the Beverly Hills Hotel. You know the kind of money that guy's making with half your talent?

LENNY So Ernie's in show business with all the other comics, and I'm trying to support my daughter . . . filling in between strippers. (*Phone again.* LENNY *grabs it crazily.*) Now what?

OPERATOR Mr. Bruce, I have a collect call from a . . .

LENNY Agghnnnnnn . . . get me outa here. (*Starts to scream into the receiver and then throws the telephone violently.*)

WOMAN'S VOICE ON P.A. Ladies and gentlemen . . . Anne's 440 is proud to present the marvelous new satire of Lenny Bruce. (*A small club forms.*)

LENNY I really hate the phone company. It's a monopoly. Where you gonna go without them? If you get too hot with the phone company you end up with two dixie cups and a thread. Chicks who work for the phone company . . . I can see them . . . their names are Terry, Winnie and Midge . . . and they wear cotton pants from Kresge's with the days of the week on them . . . right? But always the wrong day. Tijuana is the greatest place in the world to make phone calls. "Hello, Telefonicas a Tijuana" . . . "Yeah, I wanna call Beverly Hills . . . I want Crestview 4–9678" . . . "Okay, that's going to be seng dollars and fifty caints" . . . "Oh" . . . "Whads de madder" . . . "I only have four dollars" . . . "Put eet een" . . . They'll take anything . . . Chiclets . . . a sweater . . . And now, a word about dikes. Dike, as you know, is vernacular for lesbian . . . and it's strange that dikes have never received any approval in our society. I like dikes . . . Will Rogers once said that: "I never met a dike I didn't like." But it's weird, because you never see any dikes on big time TV. None that you can recognize. They're always backstage with the earphones on . . . "Ready on camera three . . . take camera two" . . . Tattoos on the thigh . . . Tony and Frank. Those you know, but it's hard to spot dikes, 'cause sometimes we're married to them. Go into your wife's closet in the afternoon . . . There's a leather Con Ed suit, with a helmet, steel boots . . .

(HUSBAND) What's this, honey?

(WIFE) It's my bowling outfit . . . keep out of there.

(HIMSELF) Comics will do endless faggot jokes, as opposed to dike jokes . . . and the reason for that I figure is 'cause . . . dikes'll really punch the shit out of you. Eisenhower . . . I've been thinking a lot about the presidency lately. That's a tough job.

Physical gig. A young man's job. Even a thirty-year-old President would be better because . . . here's the parallel . . . you want to take a chance on a man over fifty-five when Mutual of Omaha won't? And that's just for a policy. This is the presidency. And, like . . . what really upsets me is . . . here it is 1958 . . . and that's still two more years of Ike and Nixon . . . and if the Pres don't make it out of the hospital . . . (*Whistles "oh oh"*) . . . think about that for a while . . . I'd like to get a tape recorder into the White House and find out what really goes on over there. Ike. Nobody listens to his war stories anymore. (*Somewhere during this,* IKE *appears and does what* LENNY *describes.*) He just . . . wanders around the office . . . practices saluting in the mirror . . . tries on his old jacket . . . does a little putting . . .

(IKE *takes over.* LENNY *vanishes.* IKE *walks around with a golf club mumbling to himself.*)

IKE   I don't know what the hell to do . . . The students keep bugging me about the bomb . . . I don't even know where the hell they keep the bomb . . . I don't know where anything is . . . This whole White House is a shithouse . . . They steal silver . . . linen . . . Keep slipping those headlines under my door every morning . . . (*Like a parrot.*) "Recession. Recession. He got us into a recession." I gotta get the heat off me and onto somebody else, that's all. (*A sudden idea.*) I know. Nixon. They threw rocks at him in Caracas and it made headlines for a week. Maybe . . . if I sent him to . . .

Lebanon . . . (*Into intercom.*) Ceil, send in Nixon. (LENNY *is carried on as a ventriloquist's dummy . . . He sits on* IKE'S *lap as* NIXON.) Hello, Nix, sweetie. Siddown, baby. How's my black curly headed devil today? Get some of that twelve-year-old Scotch over there . . . little Havana, huh baby?

NIXON (*suspicious, like a delinquent kid*) What's goin' on here? Don't put me on, Ike.

IKE Nobody's putting you on. I got the hippest idea. How'd ya like to go to Lebanon?

NIXON (*terrified*) No. No more trips.

IKE Why not? You kiddin? They'll love you over there.

NIXON Nah, they won't love me there.

IKE Oh, now is that ridiculous, ha? Send my sweetie over there? Come back with a nice Moroccan wallet? Wouldn't you like that?

NIXON No. I'd rather stay home and watch the cherry blossoms blossom.

IKE Oh, don't get maudlin now. I don't understand you. You did great in Caracas.

NIXON Are you kidding? They hated me there. They spit at me . . . They threw rocks at me . . . You saw the headlines . . . "Nixon stoned in Caracas" . . . (*Starts singing.*) Caracas . . . Caracas . . .

IKE You gonna go by a few squares that didn't dig ya? I got letters from people who really like you.

NIXON I still don't wanna go.

IKE Is that a nice way to talk to me? Create a monster, is that what I did? The boy I helped? I capped your teeth . . . (*Pause.*) I capped your teeth . . .

NIXON Pull the string, schmuck . . . Look, if I just did good in one place.

IKE You did good in California.

NIXON Nup . . . I ain't got it. I think it's my hair, or something.

IKE Want to know the truth?

NIXON What?

IKE It's not you. They like you. It's your old lady.

NIXON Pat? Pat?

IKE They don't dig her, man. She overdresses.

(*The bit ends with* LENNY *alone once more. There is the indication of another club, another time.*)

CLUBOWNER Lenny Bruce, ladies and gentlemen, Mr. Lenny Bruce.

LENNY   There was one guy . . . from my childhood . . . a man who did it all for you, and wanted nothing in return. He was truly a good, good man, a man that never waited for "thankyou." Who was that good man? . . . The Lone Ranger . . . He was truly that Corpus Christi image projected, a man that never waited for thankyous. Cleaned up towns of five thousand people. Always did the same bit. The silver bullet, nod and split. *Hi Ho Silver . . .*

> (JEWISH VOICE)   Hey. What's with that schmuck? He didn't wait for thankyou, nuttin'? We made coffee and cake.

> (NEGRO VOICE)   You don't know 'bout him, man? Thass the Lone Ranger.

> (JEWISH VOICE)   What's with him he should do that? He leaves a bullet and runs. He don't want anything?

> (NEGRO VOICE)   Nothin', man. He's a verbissener. He just splits.

> (JEWISH VOICE)   That's amazing . . . not a thankyou? You couldn't give a person a thankyou? This I never heard of. We'll ambush him and find out why . . .

> (RURAL HICK)   Don' you move, you psychotic bastard. Maw, hold this gun. Hey, massed man, what the hell is yo storee? How come you never wait around for thankyous? You know these kids here made up a hamantash? And they made up a sawng, "Thank You Lone Ranger." And look at you . . . you're jus too damn good for evvribuddy,

aren't you? You just gotta run awff an never assept any love, a thank you, something. You know thass Anti Christian in spirit . . . not to assept a thankyou, some love?

(LONE RANGER) Well, I'll explain . . . if you'll get your goddamn hands off me. You see, the reason I never wait for thankyous, I figure supposing some day I do wait for a thankyou . . .

(HEARTY VOICE) Thank you, Lone Ranger.

(LONE RANGER) Whassat?

(HEARTY VOICE) I said, Thank you.

(LONE RANGER) Hmmmmmmmm. I've never had a thankyou before. I rather like it. Could I have one more?

(HEARTY VOICE) Right. Thank you.

(LONE RANGER) Just one more.

(HEARTY VOICE) What the hell, I'm not goin' ta kiss your ass all day. Thankyou thankyou.

(LONE RANGER) Now I've had my first thank you, and I dig it, so I'm riding all around: "Thankyou," "Don't mention it." "Thankyou," "Don't mention it." So a week goes by, when I've had all the thankyous I need, and somebody says . . .

(FIRST VOICE) Along with the thankyou, we'll give him a little present.

(SECOND VOICE) He wouldn't take.

(FIRST VOICE) He'll take. They'll all take. We'll give him an Esterbrook pen.

(LONE RANGER)   Well, that's the way it goes. I'm riding around getting thankyous and pens, and I dig it. Another week goes by . . . and I'm bored with pens.

(HICK)   Wall, goddamn, massed man, can't you just bend one time? Assept something good, meaningful . . . some love.

(LONE RANGER)   Awright. Gimme that Indian over there.

(HICK)   Tonto?

(LONE RANGER)   Whatever the hell that spic halfbreed's name is. Yes, Tonto.

(HICK)   Goddamn, massed man, we can't give ya a hooman being.

(LONE RANGER)   Bullshit you can't give me a human being. What did you think I was going to ask for, schmuck, a dish? Now . . . I want that Indian.

(HICK)   Awright. What the hell you wannim faw?

(LONE RANGER)   To perform an unnatural act.

(HICK)   Goddamn. The massed man's a fag. I never knew you were that way.

(LONE RANGER)   I'm not, but I've heard so much about it and how bad it is, the repression kind of has me horny, you know, I . . . I'd like to try it just once before I die. I like what they do with homosexuals in this country . . . put them in jail with a lot of men. That's good punishment! While you're at it, I want that horse, too.

(HICK) Fawwat?

(LONE RANGER) For the act.

(HICK) Gawd damn. Maw, did you hear that? . . . The massed man's a degenerate.

(LONE RANGER) Oh, yes . . . this mask. You didn't recognize me, did you? I've made many movies in Paris with a mustache and garters. Hi Ho Silver.

(HIMSELF) I wonder about the anonymous giver. 'Cause the anonymous giver truly is the man to be wary of. I'm going to leave you with this, that the only anonymous giver is the guy who knocks up your daughter. (*After a pause.*) You know, we've got to stop pissing money away on Radio Free Europe. Why? Because there's a whole nation inside our country . . . a nation of black people we know nothing about. And after all that's gone down we never give a nickel to Radio Free South . . . ever. And I've never seen a newspaper report that understood a single thing about those people. Yeah, you're still hearing things like "Would you want one of them to marry your sister?" Here's a good summation on that cliché . . .

SOUTHERN LADY I've had enough. If you think I'm gonna sit here and listen to schmook and poots and a lot of other filth that I just don't even understand . . . you're crazy. (*Picks up shotglass and tosses it at him.*)

LENNY That's a weird kinda heckler. See, those people that just left . . . they're in for a surprise . . . We all are . . . because there are a few more black people than we know about. Oh, yeah . . . because I assume census takers have been remiss in their duties, and passed a few of those houses by . . .

(CENSUS TAKER)   Ah, frig it, man. I don't want to go in there . . . I don't wanna go in them houses . . . all that dog shit and crap and dirt . . . Just don't wanna go in them houses, that's all. Ask that kid on the lawn. How many of them live on this block, sonny?

(KID)   Ah . . . well . . .

(CENSUS TAKER)   Okay . . . write that down . . .

(POLITICIAN)   Two billion votes from Alabama, and the vote's still coming in! Where're them votes coming from? Where've them people been?

(HIMSELF)   They've been living sixteen thousand to a house with bunks and tiers. And their vote's gonna bring a change. Someday soon you'll see an all black jury and a black judge and . . . shit.

(OUTRAGED VOICE)   An all black judge and jury . . . How'm I gonna get a fair shake there?

(HIMSELF)   You ain't. Haha . . . yeah . . . liberal, schmiberal . . . oh yeah . . . it's gonna be a lotta dues, Jim . . . Are there any niggers here tonight?

MEMBER OF AUDIENCE   Och! Where?

LENNY   I know that one nigger who works here, I see him back there. Oh, there's two niggers, customers, and ha, aha. Between those two niggers sits one kike, man . . .

Thank God for that kike. Uh, two kikes. That's two kikes and three niggers, and one spick, one spick, one hick, thick, funky, spunky boogy.

AUDIENCE   Funky, spunky boogy.

LENNY   And there's another kike.

AUDIENCE   Three kikes.

LENNY   Three kikes, one guinea, one greaseball.

AUDIENCE   One greaseball.

LENNY   Three greaseballs, two guineas.

AUDIENCE   Two guineas.

LENNY   Two guineas, one hunky funky lace-curtain Irish mick.

AUDIENCE   Irish mick.

LENNY   That mick, spick, hunky funky boogy.

AUDIENCE   Hunky funky boogy.

LENNY   Minus two yid spick polack funky spunky polacks.

AUDIENCE   Funky spunky polacks.

LENNY (*as* AUCTIONEER)   Five more niggers. Five more niggers.

MEMBER OF AUDIENCE   I pass with eight niggers and four micks.

LENNY   The point? That the word's suppression gives it the power, the violence, the viciousness. If President Kennedy would just get on TV and say, "I'd like to introduce you to all the niggers in my Cabinet," and if he yelled niggerniggerniggerniggernigger at every nigger he saw, boogy boogy boogy, nigger nigger nigger until "nigger" lost its meaning, its *bad* meaning, then you'd never make any four-year-old kid cry when he got home because somebody called him a nigger in school. Yeah . . . screw "Negro" . . . Oh, it's good to say nigger. Hello, Mister Nigger . . . how are you? And remember folks . . . in order to play the "Star Spangled Banner" . . . it takes both the white keys *and* the dark keys . . . Goodnight.

CLUBOWNER   Lenny Bruce, ladies and gentlemen, Mr. Lenny Bruce.

> (LENNY *appears . . . in another part of the forest, carrying a picnic basket. He puts the basket down and spreads out a little blanket. A prison* MATRON *appears with* RUSTY. LENNY *rises and goes to meet* RUSTY. *They embrace.*)

LENNY   How are you?

RUSTY   Great.

LENNY You look great.

RUSTY Yeah.

(*They run out of conversation for a moment and take out the picnic food and drink and deal with all that silently while some pretty jazz is heard. Finally, they are seated, munching on chicken legs.*)

LENNY Oh . . . I brought some dynamite pictures of the baby to lay on you.

RUSTY Oh, where?

LENNY But you gotta wipe your hands first . . . They're the best pictures I ever took and I don't want you schmutzing them up.

RUSTY What an old lady you are sometimes. (*She wipes her hands and eagerly flips the photos over.*) Oh . . . she looks so beautiful.

LENNY Do you dig the composition of that shot . . . how I used the coffee table?

RUSTY I don't care about the composition . . . let me look at the kid. Oh, Lenny . . . ha ha, that's far out, man . . . Hey where was this one taken?

LENNY Oh . . . up at Buddy Hackett's.

RUSTY You don't take her picture in any chick's places, do you?

LENNY   No. I would never do that to you, baby.

RUSTY   Just at your mother's . . . right?

LENNY   Shut up, you nafka.

(*They stare at each other a moment and kiss. The* MATRON *appears again.*)

MATRON   Your three minutes are up, Miss.

(RUSTY *and* LENNY *pack up the basket quickly.*)

RUSTY   You're really making it, aren't you, Daddy?

LENNY   Yeah. It's weird. I'm getting like . . . a following . . . and the people don't look like musicians but they're laughing at the same things that only used to crack up the band. I wonder what that can mean?

RUSTY   It means that you're just so damned funny, man.

(*She is smiling at him. She turns with the* MATRON *and goes very slowly.* LENNY *lingers alone for a moment, putting odds and ends back into the basket.*)

LENNY   Really weird. All my humor is based on destruction and despair. And like . . . if the whole world were . . . tranquil . . . without disease and violence . . . I wonder where I'd be? I know where I'd be . . . I'd be standing on the unemployment line right in back of J. Edgar Hoover and Jonas Salk.

(*A* BUSBOY *comes and grabs the basket from* LENNY. CLUBOWNER *comes in with backstage mike. A club lights up.*)

CLUBOWNER Hey Lenny, Lenny, there's a line right around the block.

LENNY (*to* RUSTY) Be good, baby.

RUSTY Bye, Daddy.

CLUBOWNER Ladies and gentlemen . . . Hollywood's Crescendo presents . . . Mr. Lenny Bruce.

LENNY You know, a lot of marriages went west . . . they split up . . . in my generation. Because ladies didn't know that guys were different. You see . . . ladies are one emotion, and guys are detached. They don't consciously detach, but they do detach. Now . . . a lady can't fall through a plate glass window and go to bed with you five seconds later. But every guy in this audience is the same . . . you can idolize your wife, be just so crazy about her . . . be on the way home from work, have a head-on collision with a Greyhound bus . . . in a disaster area. Forty people laying dead on the highway . . . not even in the hospital, in the ambulance . . . the guy makes a play for the nurse . . .

(WIFE) How could you do that thing at a time like that?

(HUSBAND) I got horny.

(WIFE) You got what?

(HUSBAND) I got hot.

(WIFE)   How could you get hot when your foot was cut off? People were dead and bleeding to death and dying.

(HUSBAND)   I dunno.

(WIFE)   He's an animal. He got hot with his foot cut off. An animal.

(HUSBAND)   I'm an animal, I guess. I dunno.

(WIFE)   What did you get hot at?

(HUSBAND)   The nurse's uniform, I think.

(WIFE)   He's a maniac. He got hot with his foot cut off.

(HIMSELF)   It has nothing to do with liking, loving . . . guys detach. You put a guy on a desert island and he'd do it to a coconut palm. Okay . . . so if you knew this about guys would you really be upset if you came home and found your husband sitting on your bed with a chick or a chicken . . . and want to leave . . . and that's the end of the marriage.

(WIFE)   A chicken! A chicken in our bed.

(HUSBAND)   Leave me alone, will ya.

(WIFE)   Don't touch me. You want your dinner, get your chicken to get it for you. You asshole, you.

(HIMSELF)   See, in New York it's illegal . . . "Seeming sexual intercourse with a chicken." That's the literal. How could you even fantasize that . . . doing it to a chicken? They're too short. How

*James Wigfall as The Bishop and Cliff Gorman
as The Cardinal.*

[ABOVE] *Cliff Gorman as Lenny with Jane House as Rusty.*

[LEFT] *Cliff Gorman as Lenny in his early nightclub days.*

[ABOVE] *Cliff Gorman as Lenny and Joe Silver as Lenny's fantasy of a hip swinging Judge.*

[RIGHT] *Members of the Early Early Tribe.*

Warren Meyers as Adolph Eichmann and Johnny Armen as Adolph Hitler in foreground.

could you kiss a chicken . . . they have dopey faces! I can't even imagine such a thing.

(WIFE) How come you're alone tonight? Your chicken leave town?

(HUSBAND) I don't know the chicken. I was drunk. I met it in the yard. Leave me alone, already.

(HIMSELF) Okay . . . so the marriage splits up. But who are you going to hang around with if you're divorced and over thirty? Well, you are going to hang around with chicks that are divorced. But you never can go over to their pad, because every chicken that I know that's divorced has a seven-year-old kid. It's like a prop from central casting.

(CHICK) I'd like to have you over the house, but I have a kid.

(GUY) I know.

(HIMSELF) I know I'm going to get schlepped into the bedroom, right, to look at the kid.

(CHICK) Shhhhh . . . don't wake him up.

(GUY) I don't wanna wake him up.

(HIMSELF) He's sweating there in his pajamas. Does that kill the image. Or if they don't have a kid they'll have a French poodle that wants to stay in the bedroom all the time.

(GUY) Why don't you let the dog go out?

(CHICK) He's a little dog. He's not gonna bother anybody.

(GUY) I know. I feel uncomfortable with the dog here. I mean, what's his function? What's he doing here?

(CHICK) He's looking at us.

(GUY) Pervert. Get outta here . . . I'm not an exhibitionist. Dogs make me uncomfortable. I can't do it with him in here.

(HIMSELF) Sick red eyes, tap-dancing on the linoleum. I'd rather let the kid watch. I dug your reaction . . . "Let the kid watch? That's pretty bizarre." Maybe it is bizarre, letting the kid watch . . . but assuming that it's true, that your child will ape the actions of the actor and that what he sees when he grows up he will do . . . your kid is better off watching a stag movie than *King of Kings*. Mine anyway, because I just don't want my kid to kill Christ when he comes back. And that's what's in *King of Kings* . . . But tell me about a stag movie where somebody gets killed in the end or slapped in the face or hears any Communist propaganda. And that one potential instrument of destruction that gets pulled out . . . the pillow that the guy might smother the chick with, like in the horror flicks . . . that pillow gets shoved right under the chick's ass and that's the end of the movie.

(*Fanfare.*)

CLUBOWNER Thank you, ladies and gentlemen . . . that's our second show.

(SHERMAN HART *appears suddenly with a young* CHICK . . . *his fourth wife. He scoops* LENNY *up and walks him into a dressing room and* LENNY *makes up and listens and keeps pinning the* CHICK.)

SHERMAN . . . It's just . . . you know . . . I love the younger guys coming up . . . the younger guys coming up are what make this business such a pleasure. Who the hell wants to be a parent with no children, a king with no princes. I was talking to Henny Youngman about that just the other night on Barry Gray's show . . . Happen to catch the show?

LENNY I never miss it, Sherman.

SHERMAN Hey, that reminds me. Did you hear Henny's new bit about the Ubangi who forgot to put the stamp on the letter? Actually, it's *my* bit that he caught me doing at the Concord, he just added a few . . . anyway . . . what I mean is, Lenny, you're so talented . . . I've always recognized your talent. But the things you do are so vulgar, in such poor taste. I mean, I would be ashamed to have *Time* magazine write something terrible about me and call me sick. People come to be entertained. They don't wanna hear . . . a guy wants to be able to bring his wife. You think I want to bring my little wife here to have to watch her listen to obscenities. It's not right. And . . . I'm particularly disturbed because you're a Jewish boy.

(*He gives* LENNY *a sudden smile of forgiveness and goes over and pinches* LENNY'S *face with his thumb and forefinger.*)

Aghn . . . katchkeleh.

LENNY   You know, this is why Jewish boys all end up
going to the orthodontist.

SHERMAN   See what I mean . . . you don't have to talk
dirty to get laughs. A funny bit, Lenny. Hey, hey, hey,
Lenny . . . speaking of funny bits . . . I wrote down a
bit I want you to hear . . . and this is strictly my bit, but
you can use it and it's a great great bit . . . Ain't it
honey? (*Pulls out a rancid cocktail napkin on which something is written.*)

WIFE   Oh, yeah, it's terrific.

SHERMAN   Now wait, wait till you hear this bit, Lenny . . .
because it's so funny that when you hear this you'll shit
in your fucking pants.

CLUBOWNER'S VOICE ON P.A.   Ladies and gentlemen . . .
the sick humor of Lenny Bruce.

> (LENNY *comes out onstage and works in the direction
> of* SHERMAN.)

LENNY   It was absurd, obviously absurd, but people got
upset . . . especially *Time* magazine, which labeled me
a "sicknick" . . . because I did a bit about Leopold and
Loeb and I said that the kid they killed, Bobby Franks,
was probably a snotty kid anyway. Now . . . a comedian of your generation did an "act" . . . he came out
on the stage and said "this is my act." I don't do an
"act." The audience assumes I'm telling the truth. But

what really bugs me, along with the sick comic label, is the cry of "What ever happened to the healthy comedian who just got up there and showed everybody a good time and didn't preach and didn't have to resort to knocking religion or mocking physical handicaps and telling dirty toilet jokes?" Yeah . . . whatever happened to Jerry Lewis? His neorealistic impression of the Japanese male captured all the subtleties of the Japanese physiognomy. The buck teeth that looked like the blades that extended from Ben Hur's chariot . . . repleat with the Coke bottle eyeglasses . . . that really added to the fanatical devotion the Japanese students have for the United States. And whatever happened to Milton Berle who introduced transvestism to championship bowling and upset a hardcore culture of dikes that control the field.

(BERLE)   I sweah I'w kiw you.

(HIMSELF)   Oh, the healthy comedian would never offend . . . unless you happen to be fat, bald, skinny, deaf, dumb, or blind. You know what's sick? I'll tell you what's really sick. The entertainment capitol of the world, Las Vegas, Nevada. Zsa Zsa Gabor will get fifty thousand dollars a week in that town and schoolteachers' salaries in that state . . . top salary . . . six thousand dollars a year . . . Now that's really sick . . . that's the kind of sick material I wish *Time* had written about. But we'll all have to answer someday . . . There's gonna be a Tribunal . . . They'll line us all up . . . The guy's gonna be up there in the black shrouds . . . He's gonna say . . .

(TRIBUNAL JUDGE)   Get them all up here . . . all the
performers, state their names and salaries, the sen-
tences will then be meted out. Get the first one up
here. That one . . . worshipping the bronze god of
Frank Sinatra . . . What's your name, sir?

(SAMMY DAVIS)   Sammy Davis Junior.

(JUDGE)   How much money do you make each
week, Mr. Junior?

(DAVIS)   Twenty to thirty thousand dollars.

(JUDGE)   Hmmm . . . what do you do to earn that
kind of money?

(DAVIS) (*singing*)   Time after time . . .

(DAVIS/JERRY LEWIS)   Hey . . . Dean . . . I got a
boo-boo.

(JUDGE)   Throw away his stocking cap and mezueh
. . . Twenty years in Biloxi . . . Get the next one
up here. That lady there. What is your name,
Miss?

(SOPHIE TUCKER)   So-fee Tuckah!

(JUDGE)   How much money do you make each
week, Miss Tuckah?

(SOPHIE)   Thirty to forty thousand dollars.

(JUDGE)   Incredible . . . what do you do to earn
that kind of money?

(SOPHIE)   I'm da last o' da Red Hot Mommas . . .

(JUDGE)   Burn her Jewish Records and jellies and

the crepe gowns with the sweat under the arms. Get the next one up here.

SHERMAN I've had enough. Now you stop with Sophie Tucker. (*To* LENNY *as he goes*) You're nothing but a fresh young punk. You've got a filthy rotten mouth and you got no goddamn respect for people bigger than you are. And one of these days you're gonna get it.

LENNY Listen, Sherman . . . you can't stop masturbating gradually . . . you've got to do it cold jerky. Let him go. Let the bear hump him. Did you dig the wife? Orphan Annie. Cut to . . . The House Un-American Activities Committee . . .

  (COMMITTEE CHAIRMAN) Tell me, Daddy Warbucks, what the hell you three people doing . . . you, that little girl, and that dog? Huh? Isn't it a little weird you can never see the pupils in her eyes, huh? Is it true that "Arf" really means "Next"?

  (HIMSELF) I am of Semitic background . . . I assume I'm Jewish . . . A lot of Jews who think they're Jewish are not . . . they're switched babies. Now, a Jew, dictionary style, is one who descended from the ancient tribes of Judea or one who is regarded to have descended from that tribe. But you and I know what a Jew is. ONE WHO KILLED OUR LORD! I don't know if we got much press on that here in San Francisco . . . This all happened about two thousand years ago and although there should be a statute of limitations on the crime . . . there are those who would bust us out, unrelenting dues for another deuce.

And I really searched it out, why we pay the dues.
Why do you keep busting our balls for this crime?

(TRIBUNAL VOICE)   Why, Jew? Because you skirt the
issue. You blame it on Roman Soldiers.

(HIMSELF)   All right. I'm gonna clear the air once
and for all, and confess. We did it. I did it, my
family. We found a note in the basement. It said,
"We killed him . . . signed . . . Morty." A lot of
people say to me, "Why did you kill Christ?" We
killed him because he didn't want to become a
doctor. Or it might shock a few people . . . who
are involved with the dogma . . . to say that we
killed him at his own request, because he knew
that people would exploit him. In his name they'd
do all sorts of bust out things, and bust out people.
In Christ's name they'd exploit the flag, and the
Bible, and . . . whew . . . the things they'd do in
his name. He's gonna get it if he comes back. But
. . . they're up there watching . . . Christ and
Moses . . . they're looking down and they're
saying, "What the hell are the Gideons doing with
the Bible? They're shoving it in Motel drawers.
Let's make it down to earth."

(LENNY *starts to raise his arms.* CHOIRBOYS *enter
and dress him as a* CARDINAL.)

Come on down, Christ and Moses, come on down.
And if they ever did . . . Christ would be confused, standing in the back of Saint Pat's . . . staring at the baroque interior, the roccoco baroque
interior. Because his route took him through Span-
ish Harlem and he'd be wondering what the hell

fifty Puerto Ricans were doing living in one room when that stained glass window is worth ten G's a square foot. And this cat is wearing a ring worth eight grand . . . while he's standing there conducting high mass and talking about giving and loving.

(CARDINAL)   Love, Christian love, that is nothing but forgiveness and no hostility . . . Ars gratia artis. In vino veritas. Lympho granuloma inquinale.

(*A* BISHOP *who studied with* HUGH HERBERT *rushes in and tugs on Lenny's robes.*)

BISHOP   Psst. C'mon down here a minute. I gotta talk to you. They're here.

LENNY   Get back to the Wurlitzer dum-dum, and stop bugging me.

BISHOP   Dum-dum your ass. You better get down here.

LENNY   Okay . . . put the choir on for ten minutes.

CHOIR   Sic transit gloria . . . sic transit gloria . . . sick gloria . . . sick gloria . . . alleluia . . . etc.

LENNY   Hey, putzo . . . whaddya mean running up in the middle of a bit like that?

BISHOP   Oh, it's terrible, terrible, terrible, terrible. They're here, they're here, they're really here.

LENNY Who's here?

BISHOP You better sit down, 'cause you're gonna faint. Are you ready for a shocker? Christ and Moses, schmuck, that's who's here.

LENNY Are you putting me on? Where do you see these individuals?

BISHOP They're standing in the back. Don't look now. They can see us.

LENNY Which ones are they?

BISHOP They're the ones that are glowing.

LENNY Are you sure it's them?

BISHOP I've just seen them in pictures, but that Moses is a dead ringer for Charlton Heston.

LENNY You better get me Rome quick. What the hell do they want here? Why did they come back now?

BISHOP Maybe the Jehovah's Witnesses gave them the wrong date.

LENNY No. I don't think so. Hurry up with Rome. Well, we're in for it now. Goddamnit. Did Christ bring the family with him? What's the mother's name? Mary Hail . . . ? Hurry up with Rome. If we just cool it, maybe we can talk to them. Just don't tell anyone they're here. Oh, no . . . who copped out they're here?

BISHOP   Why?

LENNY   Why? Schmuck, look at the front door.

(*The* LEPERS *appear and congregate near* CHRIST *and* MOSES.)

BISHOP   Oh . . . Christ. Lepers.

(LEPERS *begin to advance on* LENNY *and* BISHOP.)

LENNY   Hurry up with Rome. I'll try to bullshit the lepers. (*Cheerful voice.*) Hello there lepers, how are you? (*Sings.*) Hello, young lepers, whatever you were . . .

BISHOP (*handing* LENNY *the phone*)   I've got the Pope on the line, but he says to keep it to three minutes.

LENNY   Hello Johnny, what's shakin', baby? . . . Listen . . . Christ and Moses dropped by . . . and . . . hang on a minute . . . (*To the* LEPERS.) Hey . . . hey . . . nothing personal . . . just don't touch anything, all right . . . I mean, no offense, but you might catch something from us . . . Let's all go outside and get some air, huh? (*Back to phone.*) Oh, Johnny, before I forget . . . Thanks for the pepperoni . . . (*To* LEPERS.) Listen you people . . . you wanna pick up your noses, your feet, and your arms and split. Who are you waiting for . . . Saint Francis? It's just a bullshit story. He never kissed any lepers . . . He danced with two Merchant Marines and we threw him out of the Parish.

(*A* LIFE REPORTER *confronts* LENNY.)

LIFE REPORTER We're from *Life* magazine and we want to know if that's really them.

LENNY Just a moment . . . Hey sonny . . . you want to get off my hem here?

LIFE REPORTER Are they gonna heal the sick or what?

LENNY I don't know . . . I'm on the phone . . . Ask them if they're gonna do a few bits . . . (*Into phone.*) Hang on, Johnny, will you please . . . (*To* LEPERS.) Listen . . . nobody is gonna kiss you here or nothing. I mean put yourself in our place. Would you kiss a leper? What the hell are you gonna get outa that. You try to kiss 'em and they fall apart on you. (*Into phone.*) Johnny . . . will you do something fast, huh? What the hell are we paying protection for? I dunno . . . all I know is I'm up to my ass in crutches and wheelchairs here . . . (*To* LEPERS.) Listen, can't you be nice, you people? You know how Ben Hur's mother and sister got leprosy, don't ya? They just didn't put any paper down on the seats, now haul ass, will ya? (*Back to phone.*) Johnny, will you get here fast and straighten this out . . . oh, and, listen . . . Billy Graham says can you get him a deal on one of them Dago sportscars. What? What? No . . . nobody knows you're Jewish. (*Hangs up.*)

(*Whole bit fades out.*)

CLUBOWNER Lenny Bruce, ladies and gentlemen . . . Lenny Bruce.

(*Club is empty. A* PLAINCLOTHESMAN *appears.*)

PLAINCLOTHESMAN   Are you the owner here?

CLUBOWNER   That's right.

PLAINCLOTHESMAN   Did you hire this Lenny Bruce?

CLUBOWNER   Yes.

PLAINCLOTHESMAN   Well, I just want you to know that if this Lenny Bruce uses any four-letter words or ever makes fun of religion again . . . your license is in danger . . . do you understand?

CLUBOWNER   Yeah. I understand.

> (CLUBOWNER *leaves in one direction,* PLAIN-CLOTHESMAN *leaves in the other.* LENNY *appears suddenly in helmet and flying goggles, high in the air, piloting a huge prophylactic that has the letters H-I-N-D-E-N-B-E-R-G written on the side.*)

LENNY   Why, it's the Hindenberg! Smoking in the outer lobby only, please, in the little theater off Times Square . . . starring Barbara Luddy and Les Tremaine . . . It's intermission time!

act two

☆ ☆ ☆ ☆ ☆

The early TRIBE *again. They "Yadda Mop" their way into a position that bears some resemblance to people at a trial.* HEAD TRIBESMAN (SHERMAN) *is up high as a* JUDGE.

LENNY *sits apart, guarded by a* WITCHDOCTOR. *His mouth is covered with a gag and he is tied up with ropes.*

JUDGE Okay . . . now, here's the deal. You people of the jury have got to decide. Now, the defendant is charged with violating section 311.6 of the Penal Code of this tribe which provides. (*He begins chanting in an Orthodox Jewish manner.*) Every person who knowingly sings or speaks any obscene song, ballad, or other words in a public place is guilty of a misdemeanor. (*Spoken.*) Okay . . . now obscene means to the average person . . . (*chanting again*) . . . applying contemporary standards, the predominant appeal of the matter, taken as a whole, is to prurient interest; that is, a shameful or morbid interest in nudity, sex, or excretion which goes beyond the customary limits of candor in description or representation of such matters and is matter which is utterly without redeeming social importance. (*The* TRIBESMEN *are so caught up in responsive chanting that the* JUDGE *gets annoyed and turns to* SECOND TRIBESMAN.) Hey, can we get some decent jurors around here? I mean, these Rites of

79

Spring dropouts don't make it, man. Now pay attention here. This is it in a nutshell: Before you decide "guilty" or "not guilty," you've got to figure out if *that word* he said . . . in the context in which he said it . . . was completely without artistic or social merit . . . and if, indeed, the word got you *horny,* okay?

A TRIBESMAN   Well, could we have him repeat that word he said . . . in the context in which he said the word. (JUDGE *indicates they should take Lenny's gag off.*)

JUDGE   Why, sure, okay. All right Lenny . . . go ahead.

LENNY   Okay. What I said was . . . I was talking about some faggots who were busted, deviates. They were schoolteachers. And the Hearst papers in San Francisco were incensed . . . They wanted to know how come that these faggots . . . they're convicted . . . but now they're teaching school again . . . How come the school board didn't chuck 'em right off. Well . . . I said . . . there were two schools of thought . . . one, that perhaps they're good teachers, that's why they're still teaching school, and, two, there hadn't been an incident reported where a kid came home and said . . . "Today in school I learned five minutes of geography and ten minutes of cocksucking."

TRIBE   Yadda yadda yadda, etc.

JUDGE   Okay . . . all right . . . oh boy . . . okay . . . let's get a verdict and get out of here. Oh, oh.

(*The* TRIBE *goes to deliberate.* CLERK *gets a piece of slate with their verdict.*)

CLERK   We the jury find the defendant not guilty of the offense charged, misdemeanor, to wit . . . violating section 311.6 of the penal code of this here tribe. Ladies and gentlemen of the jury, is that really your verdict?

JURY   Yes.

JUDGE (*to* LENNY)   All right. Do you desire the jury polled? (LENNY *shakes his head.*) Listen . . . would you go ask them if that's really their verdict?

CLERK   Ladies and gentlemen of the jury, is that really your verdict?

JURY   Yes.

CLERK   Yes.

LENNY (*ripping off the gag*)   Is that weird? It's like he's saying, "Are you sure?"

TRIBE   Yadda yadda yadda yadda, etc.

(*The scene segues to a presentation of Lenny's house atop Hollywood Boulevard. Many are revealed to be in bathing suits.* LENNY *and* RUSTY *kiss.*)

SECRETARY   Lenny . . . Lenny. Come on. The plane is going to leave without you.

JUNKIE MUSICIAN   Hey, Lenny . . . did Rusty tell ya what we're holding?

LENNY   Yeah, but look . . . I gotta pass on two counts, man. My doctor and my lawyer. You know what I mean. I gotta cool everything now.

NOD-OUT MUSICIAN   Hey, no panic, pops. Like if you change your mind you know where to reach me.

> (*Everyone fades out except* RUSTY, *who comes to him with a raincoat and puts it on him tenderly.*)

RUSTY   You better take it, man. Chicago is a cold, cold town. (*She is gone.*)

> (LENNY *stands alone. His stage appears. He has lost the energy and the thrust of the previous scene. He looks disturbed. Picks up the mike and performs a little benediction with it, saying to the audience with a smile:*)

LENNY   Bless you, bless you, bless you. That's because you were good. Ah . . . the reason I'm wearing my rain-coat tonight . . . as most of you know . . . I've been getting busted a lot lately . . . and . . . I've been told there are Peace Officers here in the club . . . so . . . ah . . . the last two times I was busted . . . San Francisco and L.A. . . . they didn't let me get my coat . . . and since Chicago is cold . . . if they come . . . I'm ready . . . Yes . . . there they are . . . five . . . There's the state heat, the county heat, the city heat, and two guys from Interpol. Okay . . . I was first arrested for obscenity in San Francisco a little over a year ago . . . and there's been a lot of confusion about the trial . . . mainly because of the press . . . so I thought tonight I'd lay a little of this on you because it's pretty surreal . . . okay . . . I was arrested for using a ten-letter word . . . I'm not going to say the word tonight, but you all know what it is . . . ten letters . . . begins with a c, ends with an r. They said it was vernacular for a favorite homosexual practice, but I don't relate it only to homosexuals . . . I relate it to any contemporary woman I know, would know, would love or marry . . . but they're hung up with faggotry. All right, so the scene was . . . Dirty Lenny . . . Dirty Lenny said a dirty word and I got shlepped away for it . . .

(*By now something has happened with the set so that it is clear that* LENNY *is doing the bit for us and that he is not being arrested right there at that moment in Chicago. Two* COPS *have grabbed him.*)

FIRST COP   Listen, Lenny, I'm sorry, but did you say what I thought you said up there?

LENNY   I said alotta things up there.

FIRST COP   Yeah . . . but that word.

LENNY   Oh. Yeah.

FIRST COP   Well, Lenny . . . it's against the law. I'm gonna have to take ya downtown.

LENNY   Okay. That's cool.

FIRST COP   Yeah, see . . . because it's against the law to say it and to do it.

LENNY   I didn't do it.

FIRST COP   I know, but ah . . . I just have to tell you that.

LENNY   Okay. (*He is being fingerprinted.*)

SECOND COP   You know that word you used? I got a wife and kids . . .

LENNY   I don't wanna hear that crap, man. I don't want to get involved emotionally in this.

SECOND COP   Whaddya mean you don't wanna hear that crap?

LENNY   I don't wanna hear any of that shit man, that's all. I don't want to get involved in personalities. Unless you're that kind of husband that is that loving that he shields his wife from every taboo derogatory phrase. Or are you that kind of husband that just keeps his old lady knocked up and chained to the kitchen and never brings her a flower and does raise his hand to her and does rap her out. But if I say "shit" in front of her you'll punch me in the mouth . . . that kind of chivalry, man. Did your wife ever do that to you?

SECOND COP   Never.

LENNY   You ever say that word?

SECOND COP   No.

LENNY   Never said it? Honest to God you never said it?

SECOND COP   Never.

LENNY   How long you married?

SECOND COP   Eighteen years.

LENNY   Did you ever chippy on your wife?

SECOND COP   Never.

LENNY   Never . . . one time in eighteen years? You never chippied on your old lady?

SECOND COP   Never. (FIRST COP *prepares* LENNY *for mug shot.*)

LENNY   Then goddamnit I love you. Because you're the kind of husband I would like to have been. But if you're lying, you're going to spend some dead time in purgatory, man. "Let ye cast the first stone."

D.A.   All right, all right . . . what'd he do?

SECOND COP   He said . . . (*Whispers to* D.A.)

D.A.   No!

(*A* JUDGE *appears.*)

JUDGE   What was that . . . what did he say?

D.A.   Your Honor, he said . . . blah-blahblah.

JUDGE   He said blah-blahblah?

ARRESTING OFFICER   That's right. I couldn't believe it. Up
on the stage in front of women and a mixed audience,
he said blah-blahblah.

JUDGE   Blah-blahblah. This I never heard. He said blah-
blahblah?

ARRESTING OFFICER   I wouldn't lie to you, Your Honor.
He said blah-blahblah.

D.A.   Oh yes, he said blah-blahblah. Look at him. He's
smug. He won't repent. He's glad he said blah-blahblah.

LENNY (*out front*)   Now I dug that they sort of liked saying
blah-blahblah, because now they're all saying it a few
extra times.

COURT REPORTER   Hey. Wait a minute . . . he said blah-
blahblah?

BAILIFF   Why that blah-blahblah.

JUDGE   Shut up, you blah-blahblah.

D.A.   His Honor said blah-blahblah.

ARRESTING OFFICER (*yelling it at* THE COURT)   That's right.

He said blah-blahblah. Goddamn. It's good to say blah-blahblah.

EVERYBODY   Blah-blahblah. That blah-blahblah. Blah-blahblah. Etc.

LENNY (*out front*)   Okay . . . the trial. (*As he talks the courtroom fills up.*) Now I wasn't hip . . . never been arrested before . . . and I figure, "Gee . . . I'll get to pick the jury." What a groove that was because I have looked at you people for the last twelve years and have talked about everything wild and clocked you, and I can pin you, and I know what you will have some sort of sympatico with. So . . . I pick the jury and here comes one lady . . . a Roman Catholic, and I know, a deterrent to me. As a juror she's gonna make me pay some dues, but I had a lot of conflict about rejecting her . . . because I was ashamed of the prejudice I had within myself.

ARTIE   Challenge that one, Lenny.

LENNY   Oh, frig it . . . put her on. Maybe she was Eugene O'Neill's mother.

LENNY'S LAWYER   Now, would you be prejudiced if you heard any words like blah-blahblah?

(*The* CHICK *goes up the wall, turns red.*)

LENNY   Oh oh . . . (*Takes a closer look at her.*) . . . What's that on her forehead, man . . . Dirt . . . What's today?

ARTIE   Ash Wednesday.

LENNY   Oh . . . that's gonna be a lotta dues, Jim.

LENNY'S LAWYER   Well, Christ . . . she's not gonna lie. I
  mean, she's not gonna say that word got her horny, is
  she?

LENNY   Well, she might lie for the Lord. Yeah . . . 'cause
  I'm a despot, a nut, a lunatic. And what matters is . . .
  the despot must be destroyed.

LENNY'S LAWYER   But Lenny . . . you don't understand . . .

ARTIE   Hey, Lenny . . . let this guy handle it for you.

LENNY   Okay . . . keep her on. (*Out front.*) Okay, so they
  go back and forth, back and forth, what did he say and
  blah blah blah. Now dig this . . .

LENNY'S LAWYER (*concluding his opening statement*)   . . .
  and we are going to prove, ladies and gentlemen of the
  jury, that the nature of Mr. Bruce's performance on the
  night of October the fourth was in the great tradition of
  social satire, related intimately to the kind of social satire to be found in the works of such great authors as Aristophanes, Jonathan Swift . . .

D.A. (*doing* LIONEL BARRYMORE)   I'm going to object. Your
  Honor . . . Aristophanes is not testifying here, or any
  other authors, therefore, I am going to object to that at
  this time as improper argument.

LENNY'S LAWYER Your Honor, I didn't say that I would call Mister Aristophanes.

JUDGE (*also* LIONEL BARRYMORE) I don't think you really could.

LENNY . . . the judge is really keen . . . he catches everything. Dig this one . . .

JUDGE Just a moment please . . . Mr. Wallenstein . . .

D.A. Yes, Your Honor?

JUDGE Your fly's open.

LENNY (*out front as they go on and on*) And on and on . . . and blah-blah-blah . . . but the bit that really had everyone crazy . . . (*He walks down to a drum set as he talks and simultaneously a tape recorder is dragged into court.*) Four days they went on and on and finally it came down to this . . .

ARRESTING OFFICER (*on stand*) Well, he did a man and woman involved in a perverse act and accompanied himself on the drums.

(LENNY *picks up drumsticks.*)

LENNY'S LAWYER Your Honor . . . may the tape of the performance be introduced at this time?

JUDGE All right . . . but this is not to be regarded as a performance . . . this is not for your entertainment.

LENNY Now a drum solo that I've heard my whole adult life . . . and as a kid while sleeping on the mohair couch. (*As a drum solo.*) Weeellll . . . tooo is a preposition. Commmmme is a verb. To is a preposition. Come is a verb. The verb intransitive. To come. Ah ah. To come. Yeah. I've heard these words my whole adult life and as a kid when I thought I was sleeping. Yeah. Tooooo. Commmme. Tooooo commmme. Yeah. It's been like a big drum solo. Did you come? Dijacome. Dijacomegood. Did you come. Good. Didjacomegood. Didyou comegooddidyoucomegood. Come. Come. Come. Come. Come. Gooooood. I come better with you sweetheart than with anyone else in the whole damn world. I really come so good with you . . . after being married for twenty-two years . . . goddamn I sure do love you. I came so good with you . . . but I come too quick, don't I? That's cause I love you so damn much. Do you know that with everybody else I'm the best baller in the whole world? But with you, I'm always apologizing. If you just wouldn't say anything . . . yeah, just don't say, Don't come in me. That's what it is. Don't come in me, don't come in me, don't come in me mimme. Don't come in me mimmee Don't come in me mimme. Don't come in me mimme. Don't come in me mimme. mimme. mimme. Comeinme. Comeinme. Comeinmecomeinmecomeinme. Comeinme. Don'tcome inme mimme don't comeinme . . . unless you want to kill me. (*Singing.*) I can't come, don't ask me. I can't come— (*Spoken.*) 'Cause you don't love me, that's why you can't come. What the hell's loving got to do with coming. I just can't come. That's all. 'Cause I drank too damn much.

(The JUDGE bangs his gavel.)

JUDGE   Now . . . just turn that thing off a moment. There is a very serious question involved here.

(The court fades and he is once again on the stage in Chicago.)

LENNY   Now if anyone in this room or in the world . . . finds those two words "to come" decadent, obscene, immoral, amoral, asexual, if you think I'm rank for saying it, if you the beholder think it's rank for saying it, if you, like that peace officer, would go into a courtroom and describe the act "to come," as "perverse," then you probably can't come. See . . . let me explain something about obscenity . . . about "decent" and "inde-cent" . . . If you believe there is a God . . . a God that made your body . . . and that you can do anything dirty with that body . . . if you keep telling little chil-dren to cover up, cover up, that the body is dirty . . . titties are vulgar . . . then the truth is . . . the fault lies with the manufacturer and you have got to shlep God into court with me and Belle Barth. Okay all right. You wanna hear the bit? How I actually beat the rap? Remember the lady with the ashes? I was right. She got into that jury room and locked up there bitchin' bitchin' bitchin' . . .

THE WOMAN   He's guilty guilty guilty.

LENNY   . . . but it got to a point where she hadda get out of there. Why? Because she was a lush and she hadda have a drink. So I was saved by Old Overholt. Okay ... about a year later somebody wrote it up ... "Sick comic Lenny Bruce, out on bail on a narcotics charge, was arrested by a Yiddish-speaking undercover agent placed in the club two nights running to determine if Bruce's constant use of Yiddish was a cover for profanity." See ... what happens is ... if you get arrested in Town A and then arrested in Town B with a lot of publicity ... by the time you get to Town C ... they have to arrest you or what the hell kind of shithouse town are they running. Okay ... we've established the fact that we live in a society that says ... "this is clean and this is dirty." Therefore you would assume that in the entertainment capital of that society, Las Vegas, Nevada, the attraction would be the most austere. What is the attraction in Las Vegas, Nevada?

(LAS VEGAS ROTARY CLUB MEMBER) Well, at the Stardust we have the Passion Play.

(HIMSELF) All right. Then they're consistent. What follows the Passion Play?

(ROTARY BOOSTER) Well, I believe we're having a Monet exhibit, then Eugene Ormandy with the New York City ballet, and then Lotte Lenya for two weeks.

(HIMSELF) Is this the attraction that all the moralists, all the purists support in Las Vegas? No. What's the attraction? ... Tits and ass.

(BOOSTER) I beg your pardon.

(HIMSELF) Tits and ass is the attraction.

(BOOSTER) Just tits and ass?

(HIMSELF)   No . . . an Apache team and tits and ass.

(BOOSTER)   Well that's what I go to see. The Apache team. What's the second biggest attraction?

(HIMSELF)   More tits and ass.

(BOOSTER)   The third?

(HIMSELF)   Tits and ass, and more ass, and tits, and ass and tits and ass and tits and ass.

(BOOSTER)   Do you mean to tell me that *Life* magazine would devote three full pages to . . . how did you put that . . . tits and ass?

(HIMSELF)   Yes. Right next to the articles by Billy Graham and Norman Vincent Peale. *Life*, *Look*, *Nugget*, *Rogue*, *Dude*, *Cavalier*, *Swank*, *Pageant* (The Legion of Decency's *Playboy*), and millions of other stroke books . . . the antecedent to *Playboy*, *National Geographic*, with the African chicks . . . oh, yeah . . . they're stroke books. Actually it would take the seriousness out of things like the Bay of Pigs or the Cuban Missile Crisis if you could just imagine JFK in back of the bathroom door whacking it to "Miss July" once in a while.

(BOOSTER)   Ah, well, that may be the truth, but you can't just put "Tits and Ass Nitely" up on the marquee.

(HIMSELF)   Why not?

(BOOSTER)   Why not? Because it's dirty and vulgar, that's why not.

(HIMSELF)   Titties are dirty and vulgar? Not to me, Jim. I like to hug 'em and kiss 'em.

(BOOSTER)   You're not going to bait me. It's not the titties. It's the word. The way you relate.

(HIMSELF)   I don't believe you, because I believe to you it's the titty that's dirty. 'Cause I'll change the words to "Tuchuses and Nay Nays Nitely."

(BOOSTER)   Hmmm. That's a little better.

(HIMSELF)   All right, let's make it very austere. Latin. "Glutius Maximus and Pectoralis Majoris Nitely."

(BOOSTER)   Now, that's really clean.

(HIMSELF)   To you, schmuck, but it's dirty to the Latins.

(BOOSTER)   Well then, how about something patriotic? "The Most American Girls in the World."

(HIMSELF)   American tits and ass? Grandma Moses' tits and Norman Rockwell's ass. Yeah . . . see . . . it's not the word that people feel is dirty . . . it's the titty. If the titty is bloodied and maimed then it's clean. But if the titty is pretty then it's filthy. That's why you never see any obscenity photos that are atrocity photos. Um um. If the titty is cut off and distended, that's good. Yeah, it's really weird. (*The* COPS *make a sudden move.*) Ughn . . . oh . . . here we go again.

FIRST COP   All right, folks . . . the show is over, Lenny.

LENNY   Ha . . . it's fun time.

SECOND COP   Would you please get out your I.D.'s.

LENNY Oh . . . this time the whole audience gets
shlepped away for *listening* to an indecent show.

FIRST COP . . . Let's go.

LENNY (*yelling, as a* D.A.) Misses Dolan . . . you mean
the man said motherfucker and you just kept sitting
there? . . . well, I think sixty days on the work farm
isn't going to hurt you at all.

A GIRL IN THE CLUB AUDIENCE Oh . . . I don't have my
I.D. with me.

SECOND COP Please have your I.D.'s out where I can see
them.

(LENNY *gets dragged offstage.* CHICK WITHOUT I.D.
comes up out of audience and confronts COP.)

CHICK WITHOUT I.D. Hey, if you people don't get off my
ass with this I.D. bit—you're gonna hear some words
from this stage that Lenny Bruce hasn't even heard *himself* . . . I mean my father happens to be very tight with
Mayor Daley *and* JFK . . . *and* Bobby . . . *and*
Peter Lawford . . .

(*She's got the* COP *off. From the opposite side a hospital bed comes in preceded by a* NURSE. LENNY *lies
on bed. After a moment* SALLY *appears. She watches
him. He appears to be asleep. She sits down on the
bed. After a moment he wakens.*)

SALLY How do you feel?

LENNY   Well, I used to think that pellagra was about the hippest disease you could have . . . but pleurisy . . . that's . . . pretty hip. How's the baby?

SALLY   Fine. (*Silence. A beat.*) Are you going to New York?

LENNY   Yeah. Cafe Au Go Go.

SALLY   In spite of the warning?

LENNY   Sure.

SALLY   Lenny. I never thought I'd be the one to say it, but . . . pay the two dollars. Just . . . cool your act in New York a little 'till this all blows over. You got thousands of bits you can do that they can't possibly object to.

LENNY (*with a smile* . . . *as* FRANK DELL)   I got a lotta bits. I'll do all different bits.

(HIMSELF)   Nada. Can't.

SALLY   Why not?

LENNY   Because I've figured something out. This is not an isolated thing. Town A. Town B. Town C. They're really out to shut me up. And I don't see why I should let them.

SALLY   "Them." Them is very paranoid, Lenny.

LENNY   "Them" is very powerful, Sadie.

SALLY (*puts her hand on him for a moment and says, with love*) Stubborn schmuck.

>(LENNY *covers her hand with his. He gets out of the bed wearily and with great effort, and starts to make his way towards his stage, talking all the while . . . pushing . . . pushing his message out front.*)

LENNY See . . . I started getting into trouble when I picked on the wrong god. If I had picked on the god whose replica is in the whoopee cushion store . . . the Tiki God—the Hawaiian God, those idiots—their dumb god—I would have been cool . . . (*He is not on his stage yet and as he talks two uniformed* COPS *put him "up against a wall" and search him intimately as he keeps talking.*) If I would have picked on the god whose belly is slashed—he's a bank—The Chinese—those idiots— their yellow god—but I picked on the Western God . . . the cute god . . . the in-god . . . the Kennedy God . . . and that's where I really screwed up . . . And what's weird is . . . (*The* COPS *have taken most of his clothes off and are searching his armpits, his anus, everything.*) . . . if you check the record . . . no citizen ever filed a complaint against me . . . They either walk out or throw old-fashioned glasses at my head . . . So—every case has been initiated by the Police Department . . . ah ah . . . But *you're* the ones . . . that arrested me . . . *You* are . . . *We* are the lawmakers . . . *We're* the ones who make grand juries . . . who indict . . . and I'm just somewhat weary of phony narco busts . . . Sure . . . they always end up acquitting me, but it . . . psheww . . . whacks me out financially . . . But okay . . . My decision not to pay the two dollars . . . my decision to

pay the dues . . . But the foremen of grand juries are
people who believe in bullshit . . . (*By now the* COPS
*have left him practically naked. He has reached his stage
and glares down at his audience.*) . . . see . . . because
we live in a "what should be" culture instead of a "what
is" culture . . . dig what I mean . . . I'm sure you all
saw *Time* and saw the dirty pictures of the whole Kennedy assassination . . . Now I say those pictures are
dirty because the captions are trying to bullshit everybody that his old lady is running for help or trying to
help the secret service man aboard . . . when everybody
knows that she did the normal thing . . . She probably
heard the guy yell, "He's been shot . . . let's get the hell
out of here," . . . and she tried to get the hell out of
there. But they want to teach bullshit. They want my
daughter, our daughters, if their husbands get shot
someday . . . and if they try to haul ass, save their asses
. . . they'll feel guilty and shitty 'cause they didn't stay
like that good, good woman . . . And fuck it, man . . .
she didn't stay . . . The people don't stay . . . (*He dries
up suddenly.*) . . . Aghn . . . where the fuck was I . . .
let's see . . . ha ha . . . "He's bottled out" . . . No . . .
was I doing "Snot?" . . . No . . . ah . . . Ruby . . . Os-
wald . . . Oh, yeah . . . okay . . . The foremen of
grand juries . . . are the people who believe in bullshit
. . . this kind of bullshit:

(FOREMAN)   Goddamn it, I'd never sell my country
    out.

(HIMSELF)   Have you ever been tested?

(FOREMAN)   No, but I'm just not the kind of guy that
    would, that's all. No. I'm a good American. I'd

never sell my country out. That's why I'm gonna cast the first stone. That Francis Gary Powers. He sold his country out. Gave the Ruskies them secrets. No good. Wrong guy. He's a bad apple. If I get on the jury, I'm gonna burn his ass. Send him away for a long time. That's it, no bullshit. I've got the secrets right here. I'm a loyal American. They got the other guy? They got his pants down? But I don't give a goddamn what they do to him, I'd never sell . . . What're they putting a funnel in his ass for? Can't put a funnel in his ass. Geneva Conference. Tell 'em to take the funnel out of there . . . They can't do that . . . What're they heating up that lead for? Forget it with those tricks. You ain't getting no secrets from me. They wouldn't put hot lead into that funnel that's in that guy's ass, now, would they? For a few dumb secrets. Would they? Would they? . . . They would . . . Well, that's ridiculous. Oh, the secrets? Here they are, buddy. I got more secrets, too, you wouldn't even believe. These are bullshit secrets. I'll make up shit. I'll give you the President and the White House. I just don't want hot lead in my ass, that's all. It's just, ah . . . fuck you. You take the hot lead enema. Are you kidding? I just don't like hot lead in my ass, that's all. Yeah. Had it once, didn't agree with me. We got a million secrets. What the hell's six hundred secrets, for Chrissakes?

(*A* COP *materializes suddenly on the stage.*)

COP All right, Lenny . . . you are in violation of 1140a of

the Penal Code of the State of New York . . . "Giving
an indecent performance" . . . and . . .

LENNY (*yelling wildly*)   See . . . they just don't understand
. . . they just don't know that there's a difference between a big piece of *art* with a little *shit* in the middle . . .

> (*The* COP *deposits him in an area where* ARTIE *stands
> with a* DISTINGUISHED *obscenity* ATTORNEY.)

LENNY (*still yelling*)   . . . and a big piece of *shit* with a little *art* in the middle . . .

ARTIE   Okay, Lenny, all right man. Just cool it. Just cool
it.

LAWYER   No. I'm not going through this with you one
more day.

LENNY   One more day??? Hey, it's been four years for me
now . . . and I hate to bug you baby, but the boat's sail-
ing and if you lose this case I gotta do the time.

ARTIE   Lenny, if you'll just listen a minute.

LENNY   No, I want to testify. That schmucko license com-
missioner is in there doing my act and he's *bombing* . . .
Now I wanna do the show . . . I wanna testify for the
court.

LAWYER   Lenny, believe me—the appellate court . . .

LENNY There's two thousand errors in the transcript. Look . . . I said "Person's houses and papers" and they've got "Pussies, hoses, and rapers." What the hell is the appellate court going to think when they read this?

LAWYER You won your case in Chicago on appeal and there's no reason why . . .

LENNY But that took two fucking years and everything I had in the bank. You people don't understand. I'm like a nigger in Alabama lookin' to use the toilet and by the time I get the relief it's gonna be too late. Now goddamnit. Either let me testify and do my act for the court or I'm gonna put a lien on the files and sue your ass.

LAWYER You want to be an attorney? You want to go in and work the court? You want to play the big room, Lenny? Fine. I've had it with you.

(*He walks away angrily, dropping huge law books and countless recorded tapes to the floor.* ARTIE *goes after him.*)

ARTIE Hey, wait a minute. Let me talk to you.

(*He is gone.* LENNY *wanders into an area that represents his house, and tries to put the tapes, legal papers, and books together as he laughs and talks.*)

LENNY They don't understand. I just can't make my attorneys understand. Dig what happens. I do my act at let's say eleven o'clock at night . . . Little do I know

. . . eleven o'clock the next morning another guy's doing my act who's introduced as Lenny Bruce . . . in substance . . . "Here's Lenny Bruce . . . in substance." Now, a Peace Officer who's trained to recognize clear and present danger . . . not make believe . . . goes in front of the Grand Jury . . . does my act . . . They watch him work and the Grand Jury goes . . . "That's disgusting." But *I* get busted. And the irony is . . . I have to go to court and defend *his* act.

(*A* PEACE OFFICER *appears, walking hastily down a hall and he is accosted by a* D.A.)

D.A.   Hey . . . come here . . . Now you're going to do Lenny Bruce's act in six weeks in front of the Grand Jury.

PEACE OFFICER   Wait a minute . . . I'm no comedian . . . What kind of a script . . . Do I get any direction?

D.A.   Just take this pencil and this pad and go down to the club and steal his act.

(*The* COP *starts pacing.*)

LENNY   Okay . . . now the cop has stolen my act and he's in the hallway outside the courtroom waiting to go on . . . He's nervous . . . He's sweating . . .

PEACE OFFICER   . . . Okay, I got that bit down pretty good . . . Oh, I'm not gonna get any laughs . . . I know it . . .

LENNY   Okay . . . now he's in front of the judge, doing my act.

PEACE OFFICER (*reading*)   Ah, Your Honor . . . here's Lenny Bruce's act . . . ah . . . let's see . . . President Kennedy jacked off during the Cuban missile crisis . . . and then his wife hauled ass to save her ass . . . and, ah . . . oh, this is a good one . . . the Lone Ranger wanted to freak with Tonto and a horse and . . . ah . . . I have to refer to my notes a minute . . .

LENNY   Yeah . . . see . . . I keep having this persistent vindication fantasy . . . that one day . . . I'm gonna walk into a courtroom . . . and this is what I'm gonna hear . . .

PEACE OFFICER   . . . and ah . . . then he made gestures of masturbation with his mike . . . and ah . . . let's see . . . he said a bit about kids and dogs watching him screw a divorced woman . . . and . . . ah . . . that's about it, Your Honor. I hope you liked it.

LENNY   And in my fantasy . . . the judge turns around and says . . .

JUDGE   That stinks! I mean, you're no comedian. You may be all right for the joints or in the lounges . . . but this is the big room, man . . . so please step down . . . and bring in Lenny. I want to hear Lenny Bruce. (LENNY *goes to* JUDGE *and gives him "skin."*) What's shaking, baby? Lenny, as you know, the difficulty of judging obscenity is the problem of "is it socially re-

deeming" and does it conform to the language standards of the community now and blah blah blah . . .
Well, you see, the problem we have, as far as you're
concerned, is that most cops just aren't used to working
the smart, sophisticated rooms . . . so, Lenny . . . we
decided to give you your day in court. Because we know
. . . that despite anything that's happened . . . you've
never lost your faith in the law. And anyway . . . that's
the American way. So . . . come on up here with me,
Lenny . . . and wail!

> (*The bench rises high into the air with* LENNY *and the*
> JUDGE *sitting on it.* LEPERS *playing instruments ap-*
> *pear as do* RUSTY *and* SALLY. *Huge puppets appear:*
> *Orphan Annie, Dracula, The Lone Ranger, and*
> *Jackie Kennedy.*)

LENNY   You want me to do the bit right here?

JUDGE   Yeah, that's cool. Hey, why not play it like Judy
at the Palace?

LENNY (*sits dangling his legs over the bench*)   Ha ha . . . far
out. Okay . . . before I do my act, Your Honor, I want
to say something about judges. See . . . we lie to judges
. . . continually . . .

D.A.   Objection, Your Honor . . . he is weeding the lit-
mus.

JUDGE   Oh . . . objection overruled. Keep talking, baby.
You're beautiful.

LENNY   . . . and the judge really thinks that everyone has a haircut and a blue suit . . . and is charming. That language in the courts . . . you know . . . "I pray you." You don't say, "Shithead, come off it." Ugh ugh. We talk different in front of judges, we talk different in front of schoolteachers, in front of librarians, in front of our kids. So . . . everyone comes in front of the judge wearing a mask. And in a situation where people are resisting and angry, the judge figures, "Jesus . . . he's absolutely nuts."

D.A.   Objection, Your Honor. I cite Rosenberg versus the New York Department of Sanitation 3189Z minus four except after C in which case it only has twenty-eight.

LENNY   And I cite Manual Enterprises versus Day. 370 U.S. 478 (1962) and I raise you by Sunshine Book Co. versus Summerfield, 355 U.S. 35 (1958).

JUDGE   Oh. Outasight, Lenny. Damn. Objection overruled. Hey, you know, Lenny . . . you really should have gone into law.

LENNY   Oh, I'm into it, man . . . believe me . . . I stay up night after night studying the law . . . It's really boss.

JUDGE   (*pulls out a pack of matches and hands them to* LENNY)   You fill out this matchcover and write to these people. You're wasting your time in nightclubs.

LENNY   Hey, thanks, baby. (*Reads the matchcover.*) "Draw my ass and win a Buick."

JUDGE   Well, listen, Lenny, I'm astounded by your knowl-
edge of the law . . . Tell me . . . what was it you said
about Jack Ruby's trial?

LENNY   Oh . . . yeah . . . well it's like . . . I was talking
about Melvin Belli, Jack Ruby's attorney . . . and how
he couldn't get through to the southern jury, you dig?
Because of his accent . . . see . . . that works in reverse
. . . Like Lyndon Johnson never had a chance, man,
because of that southern sound . . . They didn't even
let him talk for the first six months. It took him six
months to learn how to say Negro.

> (JUDGE *starts to laugh and laughs so hard during fol-
> lowing that* LENNY *has to grab him to keep him from
> falling off the bench.*)

Niggeraaaooo.

   (AIDE)   Okay . . . let's hear it one more time Lyndon, now.

   (JOHNSON)   Niggeraaoo.

   (AIDE)   No. Can't you say . . . look, say it quick
   . . . Negro.

   (JOHNSON)   Okay.   Nigrao-o.   Nigernao . . . Ah
   cain't hep it . . . ah cain't say it, thass awl . . . Ah
   cain't say niggeraa. Pissin in bed, stutterin . . . Ah
   cain't . . . What the hell . . . Niggera . . . Naggra
   . . . Neegraaa . . . Lemme show my scar . . .

   (HIMSELF)   Yeah, he's completely confused.

JUDGE   Oh God . . . a funny bit.

LENNY   Yeah . . . well that whole family is cursed . . .
That wife . . . with the white flannel socks and the dress
with the zipper up the front . . . She looks at home in a
trailer park . . .

(LADYBIRD)   More butane, Lyndon . . .

JUDGE   Oh . . . stop . . . it's too much.

LENNY   Okay, listen . . . now I'd like to do what was de-
scribed in court as: "Saint Paul Gives Up Fucking" . . .
Now what I really said was . . .

D.A.   Your Honor, Your Honor . . . if it please the court
. . . there's a very interesting point here. I would like
Lenny Bruce to take the stand and show us his arms.

(*A buzz goes through the courtroom. The* LEPERS *try
to run out of the room, but are restrained by the*
JUDGE. LENNY *slowly rolls up his sleeves.*)

JUDGE   Hey, hey, fellas, wait. Cool it, fellas. No panic.

D.A.   Would you like to explain all those little marks,
bruises, and tracks?

LENNY   With pleasure. In addition to several other dis-
eases, I have a disease called Narcolepsy that causes se-
vere drowsiness. My doctor prescribed liquid amphet-
amines . . . which I take daily by means of . . .

(*He holds out his arms in a crucifixion.*)

RUSTY Hey . . . wait a minute. Oh, far out, man. No wonder you cleaned up. I could clean up that way, my-self.

JUDGE (*raps for order*) Now just a moment. (*To* D.A.) First of all . . . I happen to know that Lenny was acquitted of all that dope business. (*To* RUSTY) And as for you. Tuck your hair under your ass and sit down.

(RUSTY *does so . . . with great panache . . .*)

(ADOLF EICHMANN *enters in a glass booth.*)

EICHMANN Well, don't blame me, you freak. I was only following orders, but you, you were ordering followers.

(HITLER *enters in stilt boots.*)

HITLER Bullshit. You can't know vat it vas like. You had to be there. It was impossible. Goering running around giving himself fixes in a housedress. I didn't know vat the hell vas going on. I asked them, "How'm I doing fel-las?" And they said, "Great . . . they *love* you, man."

LENNY That's right! That's it! Nobody told you what a putz you really were, right?

HITLER No. I couldn't get that information.

LENNY Right. Who could have told you? They were all shut up and killed (*Addresses the* COURT *and the* D.A.) See, that's where it's at. That's where it is. You must not stop the information . . . because the information keeps

the country strong. You need the deviate. Make room
for the deviate. You need that madman to stand up and
tell you when you're blowing it. And the harder you
come down on the deviate . . . the more you need him.

JUDGE   Well, I don't know about the rest of you, but I'm
perfectly willing to admit that I was wrong about this
boy.

LENNY   Thank you, Your Honor.

JUDGE   All right let's get on with it then. Let's have a fast
verdict and split.

(JURY *has a fast conference.* SALLY *rises as foreman.*)

SALLY   Your Honor . . . we have a verdict.

JUDGE   Hit me.

SALLY   We find the defendant . . . not guilty . . . of
anything . . . ever!

(*Band hits it. Pandemonium. Everyone marches off
happy. The bench comes down and the puppets van-
ish. The* JUDGE *of Lenny's fantasy is disrobed as*
LENNY *rehearses a legal argument and approaches
the bench. The* JUDGE *is the same judge but the fantasy is over and* LENNY *stands alone, holding his rolls
of recorded tape, his countless legal papers and law
books.*)

LENNY (*as he approaches bench, to himself*)   1140a is being applied unconstitutionally. Gestures of masturbation can disturb the peace, could not be obscene, although perhaps a clear and present danger because it would appeal to the prurient interests of homosexuals, but adult masturbation would not appeal to the prurient interests of police, Your Honor.

POLICE OFFICER Docket 4406. Lenny Bruce. Charged with violation of 1140a of the New York State Penal Law.

JUDGE All right, Mister Bruce. You wish to say something to the Court?

LENNY . . . I would like to testify, Your Honor.

JUDGE Are you represented by counsel?

LENNY No. I am substituting for counsel, Your Honor.

JUDGE I advised you to appear today with counsel.

LENNY Your Honor, please. I can't relate to my counsel. But I won't waste any of the Court's time, I promise.

JUDGE All right.

LENNY I haven't testified, Your Honor. The merits of the case. The obscene. The moral play. You have to see the visual. May I give the gestures, Your Honor.

JUDGE Mister Bruce . . . you were duly represented by counsel and the case was concluded.

LENNY   Always. Always duly represented and duly concluded. But you have to let me testify.

JUDGE   We will not grant your application at this time to reopen the case.

LENNY   The gestures. Masturbation. They were gestures of benediction. I have the right to say "fuck you" . . . I didn't say it. Please, Your Honor . . . I so desperately want your respect. I want the Court to know my income has gone from three hundred and fifty thousand dollars a year before all this . . . to six thousand.

JUDGE   The Court urges you to be represented by counsel.

LENNY   Finally to talk to the Court. After four years of laughing. You know your children say motherfucker. "How dare you say that, Gregory?" Finally . . . I had said . . . "These counsel insane" . . . now . . . (*thumbs through papers*) . . . I must talk to the Court. They are throwing me in with a band of pornographers.

JUDGE   Mister Bruce . . . I must ask that . . .

LENNY   Your Honor, I know what obscenity means. I know more than any District Attorney . . . any city. I know obscene is a legal word like possession is. They don't have anything to do with common sense. Let me tell you the bit . . . let me do "Saint Paul."

JUDGE   I insist we follow proper procedure in this courtroom . . .

LENNY (*dropping tapes as he pleads*)   I realize I come back before this Court as Eichmann before a Jewish Judge. It's an insane thing. I just keep trying to the Court . . . to you . . . the Court. Attorneys keep telling me, "Look, this schmuck don't know anything . . . It's only a lower Court . . . They're all assholes . . . We'll win in the higher Court." That's the language. Let me do the show. Let me do the gestures. This is not a gesture of masturbation . . . BOOM BOOM BOOM with the mike for the purpose. It's the classic illustration of "I The Beholder." Now, a lot of Jews think I'm trying to hit the audience. Perhaps a lot of quasi-Catholics think that Catholics worship symbols and statues . . . not know this. I mean, you heard Dorothy Kilgallen's testimony and you know she's not going to come down here to defend some crotch-grabbing hoodlum.

JUDGE   Mr. Bruce, I . . .

LENNY   Just let me get into some of this. (*Searches through his legal briefs, tapes, and transcripts and they fall all over the place and he gropes around for them.*) Oh . . . into the shithouse for good this time . . . forget it. Okay . . . here . . . "He made gestures . . . He said, 'Jackie Kennedy hauls ass.' " (*Looks through papers.*) Where is Jackie Kennedy? Her name is not here. Ramon, jump me now . . . no . . . naturally the Court would assume . . . I have got millions of tapes. What I do. Naturally, I tape everything. That's a way of life. I tape every day of my life now. I spent about sixty-three thousand dollars in the last two years on tape recordings. I tape-recorded every day of this trial. Tape recording of the tape recording. Let me testify . . . please, Your Honor.

Don't finish me off in show business. Don't lock up
these six thousand words. That's what you're doing.
You're taking away my words. Locking them up. These
plays can never be said again. I have no job, Your
Honor. I go in and out of hospitals to get here. One lung
peeled three times. Twice coming three thousand miles.
Won't you please let me show you what the form was?

JUDGE   Mister Bruce . . . the case has been closed.

LENNIE   All right. No "Saint Paul." Just a legal argument.
1140a is being applied unconstitutionally. You see . . .
gestures of masturbation can disturb the peace. Could
not be obscene. Although perhaps a clear and present
danger because it would appeal to the prurient interests
of homosexuals. But adult masturbation would not appeal to the prurient interests of police, Your Honor.

JUDGE   (*cutting into the above*)   We must conclude these
proceedings. Mister Bruce, these proceedings must be
concluded now. Mister Bruce . . .

LENNY   I have no money left. Might I be sentenced today?
Please . . . sentence me. I can't afford to live in this
city. I can't work here. The police took away my cabaret
card and the D.A. sent the tapes to Long Island. Please,
sentence me today.

JUDGE   (*as he is rolled off*)   No. The Court wishes to have a
probation investigation. It also requests a psychiatric
evaluation by the psychiatric clinic. December 16th.
Bail continued. Parole continued.

(LENNY *stands amidst the wreckage of his case, stumbling around a floor full of unwound tapes. The black shroud flies up, revealing a Mount Rushmore of a different sort:* EISENHOWER, KENNEDY, NIXON, *and* JOHNSON. *Huge, overpowering figures.* LENNY *looks up at them and laughs.*)

LENNY Oh, yeah . . . it was granite out there. (*Stentorian voice, à la Westbrook Van Vorhees for "The March of Time."*) In the halls of justice . . . the only place you can find justice . . . is in the halls! (*He turns to survey the wreckage on the floor. He stumbles around winding up tapes crazily.*) Oh, that's the Chef Boyardee syndrome . . . ha . . . yah . . . you got real junkie coordination Schneider. Give yourself a mark in the Delaney Book . . . Schneider, Leonard A. . . . (*Suddenly comes upon a glassine packet of heroin and holds it up to the light.*) Your Honor . . . the communists are putting shit in the law books. Far out. Where the hell did I get this? Weird. (*Puts packet into his pocket. Plays with the tape some more, winding it up and making the sound of fast-moving tape, gradually slowing it down.*) Rochmonis . . . rochmonis . . . Have rochmonis for . . . Eichmann . . . me . . . Have rochmonis for the cop standing in front of the grand jury somewhere doing Lenny Bruce's act . . . have rochmonis for the attorney, standing at the bar with Lenny Bruce for a client . . . Have rochmonis for the judge . . . standing there at night in his underwear . . . begging his old lady to . . .

(JUDGE) Touch it once . . . Touch it once . . . You never touch it anymore . . .

(WIFE) Yes I do . . . I touch it a lot.

(JUDGE) No you don't . . . Now it's a big favor if you touch it . . .

(HIMSELF) Yeah . . . isn't it sad that married guys have to jack off more than anyone else . . . 'cause their old ladies don't wanna touch it anymore and they're too scared to chippie . . . Oh God . . . Have rochmonis for . . . the world . . . (LENNY *pulls the packet out of his pocket and studies it. He considers throwing it away. For some reason he keeps it. He spots something on a legal paper. He picks it up and reads.*) . . . "He made gestures" . . . "He talked about Saint Paul giving up fucking" . . . You know what that bit is . . . about the guy giving it up for the Lord . . . best man in the tribe . . . The ones who don't give it up . . . why, they're second best . . . and the one who talks about it . . . "We'll bust his ass" . . . Oh, yeah, it's been a lotta dues, Jim, lotta dues. (*Turns and walks downstairs.*)

(*Suddenly* FOUR MEN *light up. Two* DETECTIVES *and the two* NOD-OUT MUSICIANS. *The* DETECTIVES *are roughing up the* MUSICIANS.)

FIRST COP Look, seven people are dead already. All from overdoses. All from the same rotten stash.

SECOND COP And we know it was pushed by you.

FIRST COP So why not admit it before you got twenty stiffs to answer for.

FIRST MUSICIAN   Okay, okay . . . but we didn't know it
   was bad shit, honest man.

SECOND COP   All right, start writing . . . and write fast.

FIRST COP   You just make sure you give us the names of
   everybody you gave that shit to . . . so we can call them
   or find them before it's too late.

SECOND COP   They didn't know it was bad shit.

FIRST COP   No. They never do.

FIRST MUSICIAN   Hey, man . . . what about . . .

SECOND MUSICIAN   Christ, that's right. Better put his name
   down first. (*Finishes writing and hands list to* COPS.)
   Here . . .

   (FIRST COP *sees a name on the list and points it out to*
   SECOND COP.)

FIRST COP   Look at this.

SECOND COP   That figures.

FIRST COP   You want to call him?

SECOND COP   Fuck him. *You* call him!

   (*They go.* RUSTY *enters, accompanied by a young,
   long-haired* BOY *who carries a tape recorder.*)

INTERVIEWER   Rusty, I want to ask you a few questions about Lenny if you don't mind.

RUSTY   Okay.

INTERVIEWER   When did you two first meet?

RUSTY   In 1951. In Baltimore. He was playing the Club Charles and I was stripping at a place just up the street.

INTERVIEWER   What was he like when you first met him?

RUSTY   Oh . . . he was nutty. You know . . . he did a lot of crazy things and he was always doing bits to crack me up.

(COPS *and* REPORTERS *have entered. They open the Nixon part of Mount Rushmore to reveal* LENNY *dead, lying with his head draped over a toilet bowl.*)

COP   Here it is.

ANOTHER   Wanna give me a hand with this?

INTERVIEWER   Do you mind if I ask about your marriage . . . about what went wrong?

RUSTY   Well, it's hard to talk about that . . . because, you know, sometimes things just don't work out and you never really seem to know why.

REPORTER   Can we get some pictures? Could we get a better shot? Could we sit him up for a second?

COP   Okay, but make it fast.

SECOND REPORTER   What about the needle? Can we do anything about that?

COP   Okay, but I'm going in the other room . . . so I didn't see it, right?

INTERVIEWER   I never heard of Lenny Bruce until he came to Berkeley in 1965. What do you think he had that spoke so directly to my generation?

RUSTY   I don't know. He knew a lot about people, you know. I mean . . . (*she is crying and is unable to go on philosophizing*) . . . he was just so damned funny, man.

> (*Lights have faded on* LENNY *and* RUSTY. *In the darkness there is one final pop of a photographer's flashbulb and one final image of* LENNY, *his head tilted, his arms being held outstretched . . .* "Into the shithouse for good this time . . . forget it!")